VISION MANAGEMENT©

HOW TO ACHIEVE STUDENT SELF-DISCIPLINE

TEACHING SELF-CONTROL, MOTIVATION & PROPER BEHAVIOR

Diana Day

Contributor
Rick Pehrson

Production Assistants
Wendy Truelove
Charles Crofford

Unsightly Accumulation Assistants
Cole Mann
Junior Mann
Katrina Mann

Cartoons
Chris Barker
Ben Chamley

dba Diana Day Training Products
P.O. Box 472283
Garland, TX 75047 -2283
Phone (972) 278-7773
Fax (972) 278-8584
www.dianaday.com
goals@dianaday.com

ISBN # 0-9667646-6-8
Printed in the United States of America
First Printing, July 1993
Second Printing, July 1995
Third Printing, July 1996
Fourth Printing, July 1997
Fifth Printing, July 2001
Sixth Printing, July 2002
Seventh Printing, June 2003

Tables of Content

Pre/Post Test
Vision Management©

Learn And Enjoy

1. How did your parents discipline you when you misbehaved?

2. What type of discipline do you currently use in your classroom?

3. Discipline changes in this country every _____ years.

4. The first day of class there is a poster on your wall. It tells the students your ______.

5. A classroom management plan has how many parts?

6. If you know that a student will disrupt, you would want to give a p____________ before it happens.

7. What would you do if students didn't bring this to class?
   Pencil? Give them a s________.
   Paper? B_____ C__________ or R________ Box
   Book? S__________ under two conditions.

8. What would you do if a student loudly cusses another student and your Principal, Dean, V.P., secretaries, and custodians are not in the building?

9. You can't _________ a problem during a problem.

10. To motivate students to learn we need to convince them that what we teach is ______ ______ to them.

Answers: 3. Fifteen 4. PEDS(Professional Educator Dedication Statement) 5. Three (Learning Expectations, Learning Choices, Learning Incentives) 6. Pre-minder 7. Stub, Big Chief, Recycle, Share 9. Solve 10. of value

Chapter 1

Mission Possible

Giving Responsibility; Getting results

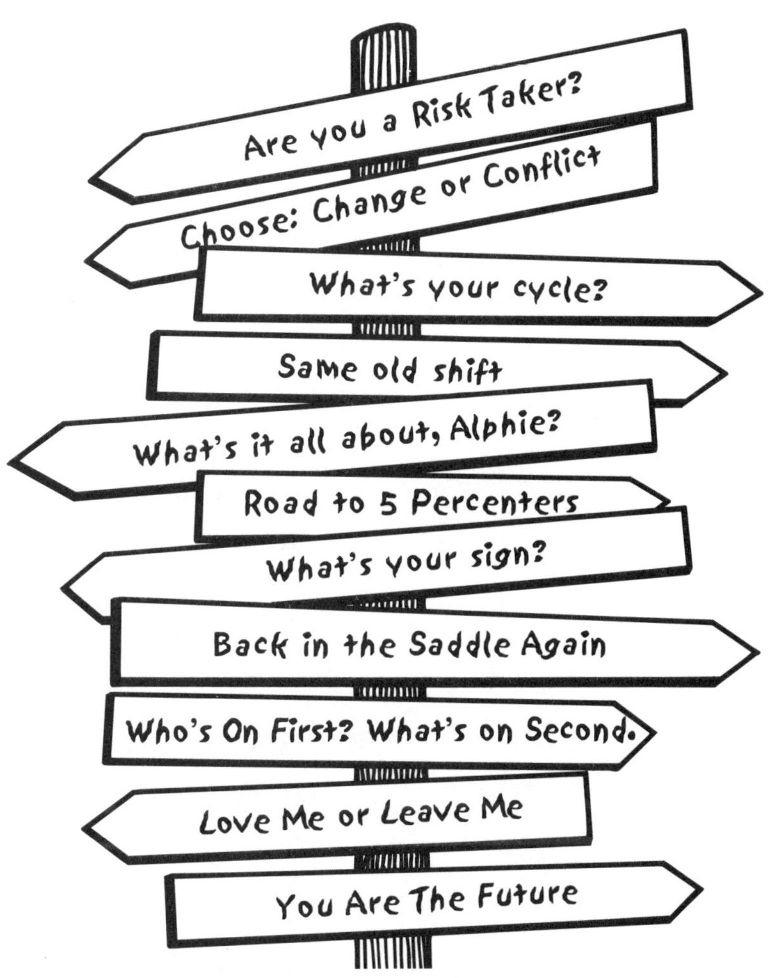

"Give students discipline and you've made your day better. Teach students self-discipline and you've made their lives better."

Vision Management© What is it?

Research-Based Behavior Management

More than merely a philosophy or attitude, *Vision Management©*, is a comprehensive, research-based program. It consists of specific brain-compatible strategies, techniques, skills, scripts and tools for successfully getting students to take responsibility and manage themselves. *Vision Management©* meshes seamlessly with existing management programs that need more substance and structure. If you want to achieve classroom-to-classroom consistency or quadrant-to-district reform, *Vision Management©* can achieve that goal.

Vision Management© is unique because it is a behavior management **system** that integrates all the component modules that address the most pressing problems faced by today's teachers. The program provides a comprehensive schoolwide discipline plan that includes:

- Brain-Based Teaching & Learning Techniques
- Whole School/District Reform
- Shared Core Values
- Character Development
- Student Self-Management
- Problem-Solving
- Conflict Resolution
- Social Skills
- Building a Community of Learners
- Staff Growth & Development

"Self-Discipline is the ultimate goal of the program."

Self-discipline is the ultimate goal of the program. *Vision Management©* teaches appropriate behavior within a structured environment, allowing students to participate in what those behaviors should be. Students help create personal performance standards in cooperation with their teachers.

Problem-Solving Replaces Punishment

Rather than monitoring misbehavior and parceling out punishment with detachment, teachers are trained to objectively problem-solve with students. This occurs in a caring, consistent fashion balanced with firmness and fairness. Students develop personal goals and participate in decisions about their achievement, accountability, safety and behavior. They help create their own learning choices, while being taught that the ultimate consequence is not acquiring an education that will equip them to achieve in life.

Success Equals Motivation & Proper Behavior

What Makes *Vision Management©* Work?

A structured environment that is positive, productive and supportive, where student expectation and achievement is high, makes *Vision Management©* work. Teacher satisfaction is heightened by specific classroom-proven approaches to successfully reach and teach today's challenging students.

Vision Management© includes specific training for parents and all school personnel from the boardroom to the bus barn. Give students discipline and you've made **your** day better. Teach students self-discipline and you've made **their** lives better.

> *"Give students discipline and you've made your day better. Teach students self-discipline and you've made their lives better."*

Are You Tired of the Same Old Shift?

A Reality Check

- Has your classroom management evolved into a potpourri of "stuff," and you still have occasional chaos?
- Are you more stressed out, handling increasingly higher numbers of unmanageable students?
- Do the old tried and true consequences for misbehavior seem ineffective?
- Do students ask, "What will you give me if I do it?"

Disenchantment & Dissatisfaction

May 1, 1993, there was a soft rain all day in Dallas. With opened windows, you could hear the steady plop...plop of drops hitting the tender, new leaves. It was a day I pondered this thought: As a teacher and educational consultant for 23 years, I had experienced vast changes in educational philosophy. Why was the method of discipline so rigid in my childhood, free-lovin' in my teaching years, evolving into check marks that doled out punishment later in my career? My disenchantment and dissatisfaction with the current management philosophy reached a peak that morning. I asked myself this question: Was there a cycle? If so, what were the markers for change? If the past were better understood, could the future be predicted? On this day, *Vision Management©* was conceived.

More of the Same Old Shift

Can the Future Be Predicted?

I began by studying what I considered to be the management philosophies of the 20th century. There appeared to be a pattern every 15 years! We have had a major shift of thinking that determined the way we taught and managed students. The students who are educated in a 15-year period with one philosophy become the parents of the next generation. The parents retain the management philosophy of their youth while their children are being managed in a new philosophical style at school. It creates disharmony. **Communication and understanding becomes a challenge between teachers and the parents of their students!**

> *"Every 15 years we have had a major shift of thinking that determines the way we teach and manage students."*

Teachers may cognitively comprehend the latest management trends but emotionally manage students from the style of their youth – a potential land mine. Now, mix parents into the equation. Teachers conference parents who are also stuck in a philosophical time warp. Acknowledging that parents are operating in a dated philosophical style will help the administrator or teacher. The clever educator, who understands the "hot buttons" that promote that style, will be able to successfully aid parents to help their children both academically and behaviorally.

Back to the Future

The markers that have created "shift" are many and varied. The **Authoritarian Shift** resulted from a backlash from the 1920's when social stigmas came down and hemlines went up. By 1930, the mood of the Depression created austere classrooms. Corporal punishment and ridicule was the course of the day. Economic times were full of fear and so were the children in their classrooms.

With the end of World War II in 1945, men returned to the industrialization of America. Women were displaced in the factories by men. Women became the teachers to the next generation of war babies. The **Parental Shift** was in the making. "Have a discussion with the little tyke about his horrible behavior" was Dr. Spock's message to parents in 1948. It set a tone of jabberwocky throughout the 50's.

In 1960, Sinatra and Como were jettisoned by John, George, Paul and Ringo. Inhale, burn your bra, don't fight for your country. The **Permissive Shift** ushered in open-space classrooms...open chaos. No more reading groups but discovery learning centers. Never say "no" to a child. It might ruin his ego, id or ishkabibble.

In 1975, when national testing results proved the U.S. was the lowest of the first-world nations in math, science and reading, someone must have dialed "911." "Take us back to the basics!" The **Monitor Shift** bailed us out. No more Mr. Nice Guy. You behave, or your buckaroo pin gets moved into the manure pile. Get three strikes and you're out, Little Buddy...and we don't discuss it.

More of the Same Old Shift

Vision Replaces Robotic Monitors

By 1990, the divorce rate was more than 50 percent. Day cares delivered and picked up the same students to and from school. We began to see the disintegration of social skills that had once been taught in the home. Parents could not be an integral part of the management system when they could not be found. The **Visionary Shift** was inevitable as it was apparent we needed to appeal directly to the child. Goals and action steps had to be created by our children for them to survive their childhood and create their future.

Is *Vision Management©* Successful?

You, teachers, believe in children. That's your business. You must not let the influence of gangs and delinquency affect your children's futures. Children are growing up amid serious social problems. The absence of healthy dialogue in the family unit may not teach your youth the desire to succeed. Few will strive to be more than what they are right now.

I created *Vision Management©* to work with a divergent school population. Students, who have been defiant, ill-mannered and aggressive, have flourished in an atmosphere that is kind, firm, fair and consistent. The school becomes the educational home for the student, where values, character formation and social skills are taught and practiced.

Discipline Cycles

The philosophy of behavior management changes as society reacts to the demands of the times. When children leave school, they become the parents of the next generation, taking their childhood-based philosophy with them.

Philosophical Shifts

	HOME	SCHOOL
1930-1945	Victim/Warrior	Authoritarian
1945-1960	Authoritarian	Parental
1960-1975	Parental	Permissive
1975-1990	Permissive	Monitor
1990-2005	Monitor	Vision Manager
2005-2020	Vision Manager	Ecommunicator
2020-2035	Ecommunicator	

Why Does Vision Work?

Referrals Down Results Up!

Schools that are following *Vision Management*© teach lessons to their students about values and goal setting to enhance their academic and behavioral awareness. Students focus on what they want to accomplish and how they plan to get there. That's in contrast to out-of-control random misbehavior. Having specific goals to set one's sights upon is the single most important factor in the improvement of academics and behavior. Achieving self-proclaimed goals is the most vital ingredient to elevating self-esteem and to producing rational decision-making.

> ***"Our Climate Survey indicated that discipline management at Dunbar was no longer a high-priority..."***

At Dunbar Junior High (Lubbock, TX), staff and administrators used *Vision Management*© to decrease office referrals by 75 percent in one semester. Assistant Principal Polly Kiker said, "This year our state scores increased more than any junior high in the city. Our Climate Survey indicated that discipline management at Dunbar was no longer a high-priority item because misbehavior had been effectively handled. That has opened the door to focus on instruction."

"Works Best with Students Needing It the Most"

Harlingen ISD's Crockett Elementary Principal, Mary Atkinson, reviewed the program at every staff meeting. "Every new staff member is trained in the program. Referrals dropped 62 percent our first year. The cafeteria is so orderly now, the PTA has put in a jukebox for entertainment."

Also, in Harlingen's Elementary Alternative Center, Principal Mary Brower said, "The main thing I'm seeing about *Vision Management*© is how perfectly it pulled together all the varying management programs throughout the district. The program has taught our teachers how to effectively help our children. Our students arrive angry and aggressive. After creating Pride Folders and setting goals, using Diana's system, our students return to home campuses with improved self-esteem and a defined purpose to meet their individual goals. Our return rate is very low.

Safe, well-managed schools are a necessary prerequisite for improving student achievement. The program seems to work best with those students who need it the most because it focuses on them in such a positive manner. Former Shackelford Elementary (Waxahachie ISD) Principal Ron Coleman summed it up by saying, "This year, we're seeing excellent results. My teachers are able to free themselves of most disciplinary problems and focus on their excellent teaching."

It's Your Choice: Manage Change or Manage Conflict!

Take a look at the concepts below to compare Stimulus-Response to *Vision Management©*.

"Are your beliefs taking you closer to or further away from your teaching goals?"

Stimulus Response-Type Discipline Programs	*Vision Management©*
Is a **Boss Manager**	Is a **Lead Manager**
Uses **Extrinsic Motivation** "You must reward me by giving me something."	Uses **Intrinsic Motivation** "I reward myself by meeting my goals."
Teacher uses **Coercive Discipline**: "I can give you pain or I can give you pleasure."	Teacher uses **Enlightened Leadership**: "I use empathetic communication & relationship-building."
Dispenses **punishment**	**Problem-solves** with student.
Student + Teacher Confrontation = **Continuous problems**	Student + Teacher Cooperation = **Focus on success**
Becomes a **Task Master**	Becomes an **Educational Guide**

Contrast

"If you don't know where you want to go, any road will do."

Is There a Risk in NOT Changing?

Any philosophical change involves risk. Risk is a necessary component when you consider changing your beliefs. Can you believe that you can give students power and it will not lessen your ability to manage them? It is a giant leap of faith. Committing to take that risk will increase your skills, build your confidence and give you unequaled professional satisfaction.

> *"We must be the change we wish to see in the world."*
>
> Gandhi

WHAT CORE BELIEFS DO I NEED TO CHANGE?

To Change or Not to Change: That Is the Question.

Discipline: From punishment-based to having students focus on their personal goals

Behavior Theory: From Stimulus Response to Vision Theory©

Management Style: From having to be the boss to feeling comfortable being the guide

Objective: From demanding blind compliance to promoting self-motivation

"The Risk"

To laugh ... that's to risk appearing the fool.
To weep is to risk being called sentimental.
To reach out to another ... why that's to risk involvement.
To expose feelings ... that's to risk showing your true self.
To place your ideas and your dreams before team members
... that's to risk being called naive.
To love is to risk not being loved in return.
To live is to risk dying.
To hope is to risk despair.
To try is to risk failure.
But risks must be taken, because the greatest risk in life is to risk nothing. People who risk nothing, do nothing, have nothing, are nothing, become nothing. They may avoid suffering and sorrow -- maybe -- but they simply cannot learn and feel and change and grow and love and live. Chained they become slaves. They've forfeited their freedom. Only people who risk are truly free.

Leo Buscaglia

Is Your Glass Half Full, Half Empty or Leaks Out the Bottom?

Is Your Auto-Responder an Energizer or a "Debilitator"?

How do you choose to look at your teaching career? Do you have a negative orientation to life or a positive one? What are the first thoughts that come into your mind when you hear something new? When a student has a request, is your brain on automatic pilot to give a negative response to shut down enthusiasm and creativity? Do you usually think of a reason why something can't work? Those are old tapes in your head from a voice in your past. Who in your past oriented you towards a negative viewpoint?

Do you look first at the price and then at the prize? What does the word "bars" mean to you?

When you think "window bars," you limit your potential. Thinking "candy bars" **widens** your perspective! **Cancel** your negative focus. Look for opportunities not limitations!

Obstacles exist only in your mind. Become a limitless thinker. What can stop you except your own fears and doubts? Change your views and change your life! The adventurer within you wants to break free of the limitations & restrictions of the past and say, "I'm free to think and do for myself! I can have fun with my students, not be embarrassed by what I say to make the lesson more appealing nor fear losing control of my students."

The greatest obstacle to change is fear.
What are things you fear?

Revive yourself through change.
Think of reasons for positive change.

Can Meeting Students' Basic Needs Help You?

Reducing Negative Behavior Improves "Vision"

Every person has five basic needs. Adults and children have the same needs. When basic needs are not being met, we get "out of balance." We say and do things we might not ordinarily do.

Meeting both teacher and student needs as a part of the ongoing educational process will prevent or reduce negative classroom behavior. If you can identify what the student or you is asking for (in some cases screaming for), you can provide experiences that will make life significantly better for both of you.

"All I need is love!"

"We cannot give what we do not have."

BELONGING	COMPETENCE	POWER	FUN	FREEDOM
Significance	Capability	Self-control	Enjoyment	Independence
Acceptance	Ability	Ability to choose	Pleasure	Self-reliance
Survival	Proficiency	Authority	Play	Self-sufficiency
Love	Mastery	Influence	Recreation	Autonomy

Are You Addressing the 5 Basic Needs of Your Students?

Grade yourself below:

Belonging ☐ Competence ☐ Power ☐ Fun ☐ Freedom ☐

5=Almost always meet this need
4=Usually meet this need
3=Sometimes meet this need
2=Usually don't meet this need
1=Almost never meet this need

What Are the 5 Basic Needs? How Are You Doing?

"Vision is the world's most desperate need. There are no hopeless situations, only people who think hopelessly.

Winifred Newman

List 3 concrete actions you could take to immediately meet your students' needs in areas that you identified.

1. BELONGING 2. COMPETENCE 3. POWER 4. FUN 5. FREEDOM

Need	Action
________	1. ______________________
	2. ______________________
	3. ______________________
________	1. ______________________
	2. ______________________
	3. ______________________
________	1. ______________________
	2. ______________________
	3. ______________________

WHAT DO YOU DO TO HAVE FUN?

TAKE A WALK ON THE WILD SIDE

You've been doing math drills for 40 minutes. It's mid-afternoon. It's stuffy and lunch was bean burritos. Your students need a "STATE CHANGE"...(that means you stop what you're doing and learn through a different sensory modality).

Ask if they'd like a 15-minute break to have...(smile when you say this), "an educational experience."

- To do this, everyone must be SILENT until they are outside
    - Once outdoors, gather class around you periodically to ask these questions:

1.) Guess the wind velocity. (Put hand in air. How hard is the wind pushing against your hand?)

2.) Guess the wind direction. After their guess, point out the afternoon sun location. Have them point where it will set. Ask what direction the sun sets. (West) Then, have all point to North-South-East-West.

3.) To determine wind direction, point out which direction the flag is flying, someone's hair is blowing, tree branches are bending.

4.) How would the weather man describe today's weather? (Partly cloudy, sunny and breezy?)

5.) Guess the temperature. (What clothes are they wearing? Are they warm, cold?)

6.) Predict tomorrow's weather.

7.) Are the trees permanently bent in one direction? What would that mean? (Wind frequently comes from that direction.)

8.) Hear any birds? What are they?

9.) What are the names of some trees, plants or flowers?

10.) For homework, watch the weather on the news. How close were all your estimates?

11.) Discuss accuracy of weather estimates the following day, having done the homework.

Excerpted from ***101 Ways to Have Fun with Your Students for FREE***© ***by Diana Day (Available Spring 2004)***

www.dianaday.com • 972-278-7773

The 80-15-5 Percent Principle

IN 1980's | **BY 2000**

1. ☐ C______________ ☐

- Rarely breaks rules
- Motivated to learn
- Successful (academically and behaviorally)
- Expects success & high achievement
- Most discipline measures are unnecessary or intrusive

List two 80%er's here ____________ student ____________ adult

2. ☐ P______________ ☐

- Can pivot up to 80% or down to 5%
- Makes affable excuses for inappropriateness
- Erratic achievement, motivation, or behavior
- Requires clearly stated expectations and consistent learning choices to conform to an 80 percenter.

List two 15%er's here ____________ student ____________ adult

3. ☐ O____ D____/C______ ☐

- Are chronic rule breakers
- Seeks to control, to have attention or is unmotivated
- Chronic failures in behavior and/or academics
- Feels hopeless, does little or no work
- Demands attention or wants no notice or encouragement

List two 5%er's here ____________ student ____________ adult

Answers: 1. 80%, Cooperative, 50% 2. 15%, Pivotal, 35% 3. 5%, Oppositional Defiant/Controlling, 15%

Geometric Logic

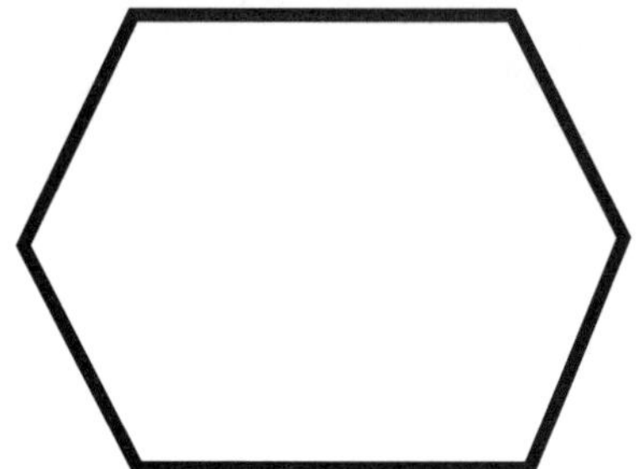

What did you see from a new angle?

What completely agreed (squared) with something you already believe?

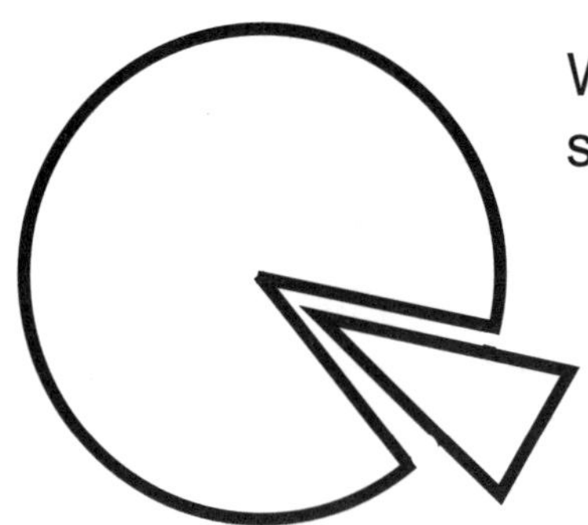

What new action can you take that compliments something you already do or believe?

What concrete action will you take as a result of this chapter?

Chapter 2

Wonder Woman and Superman Do Not Live Here Anymore

Modernizing Your Management Style

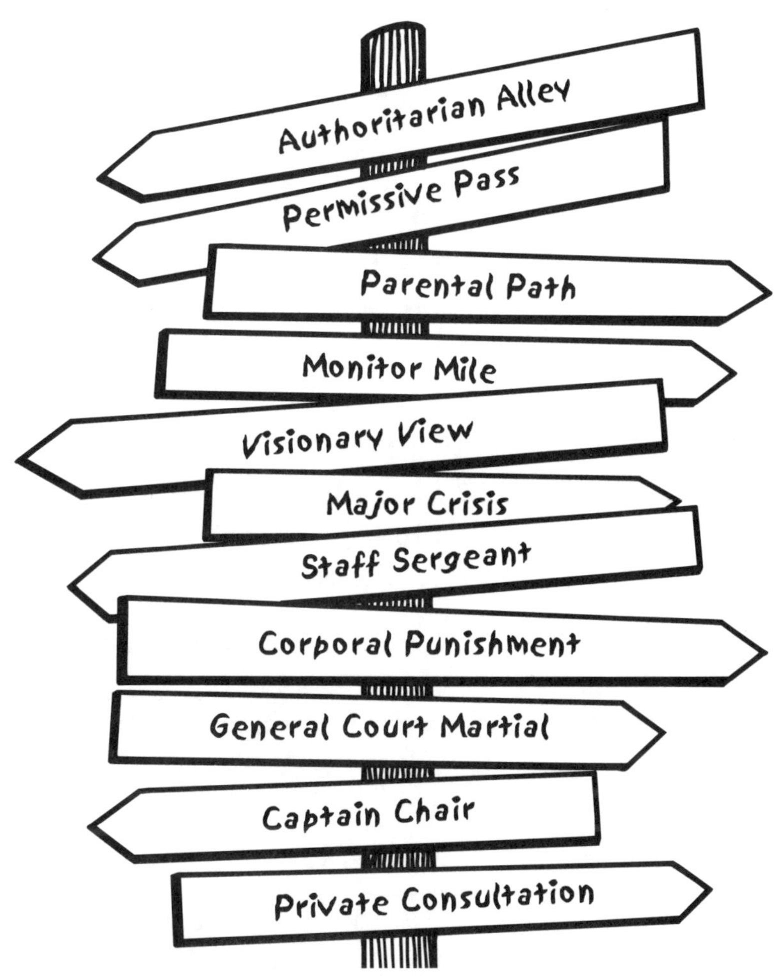

"Give students discipline and you've made your day better. Teach students self-discipline and you've made their lives better."

THE 5 MANAGEMENT TYPES WHICH ARE YOU?

The most important determinant of our classroom success is our "management style." Often we manage our students the way we were managed by our parents. Without realizing it, we may be making the situation worse and alienating students from whom we seek cooperation.

Let's look at five different management styles that are used to communicate with students, the characteristics of each, and the results they generate.

Put a mark beside each characteristic that you have used to either give direction or show/tell your dissatisfaction. Then, determine which management style **you** most frequently use.

Next, evaluate your Mother and Father's style by placing an "M" or an "F" by the characteristics that apply to them. Is your reaction to their management styles negative or positive? Is your style the same as one of your parents? Might there be a need to change your style in order to change your student's reactions to you?

1. AUTHORITARIAN

The H____________

- Punisher
- Uses Criticism
- Believes in Corporal Punishment
- Uses Intimidation, Humiliation
- Rigid Thinker
- Uses Overt Negative Control
- Overbearing
- Boss Manager

Today's students will either s_________ or r_________.

80 %ers **15-5 %ers**

2. PARENTAL

The J_________

- Nagging, Nagging, Nagging
- Uses "Silent Treatment" when Upset
- Withdraws Love & Affection
- Uses Covert Negative Control
- Focus on Mistakes from Past
- Uses Guilt, Shame, Moralizes
- Often Says " you ought to, should, have to"
- Boss Manager

Today's students r_______ and show a_______.

Answers: Hangman, succumb, rebel. Judge, reject, anger.

3. PERMISSIVE

The B________

- Makes a Joke of those who Enforce Rules
- Relies on Friendship with Students
- Fearful to Displease
- Overly Lenient, Lax
- Inconsistent w/Temporary Fits of Anger
- Overly Tolerant
- Adult Begs, "Do It for Me"
- Student Says, "I Thought You Were My Friend"
- Uses Bribery to Get Positive Control

Students m__________ & are not r_________.

Answers: Buddy, manipulate, respectful.

THE 5 MANAGEMENT TYPES

Think about the years you spent as an elementary & secondary student. Did you enjoy every grade or subject? Is your memory of the grade/subject more determined by the enjoyable, equitable interactions you had with the teacher, or merely the curriculum he/she taught?

Adults say that quality, positive interaction gets the vote!

4. MONITOR

The S__________

- Reactionary Stimulus-Response Method
- Worked in the 80's when Teachers Feared
- Boss Manager
- Admonisher
- Overseer, Counter of Bad Deeds
- Says "Three strikes and you're OUT!"
- Student Conforms to Avoid "Marks"
- Students Overtly Act-Out

Today's students will learn ways a_______ the system.

5. VISION MANAGER

The G_______

- Mentor to Students
- Focuses on Big Picture Goals
- Proactive
- Is a Good Example of High Character
- Realizes You Can't Make Anyone Do Anything
- Encourages Self-Motivation which Leads to Self-Discipline
- Teaches Students to "Never Give Up"
- Has Heart, Hope & Positive Attitude
- Strives for Student Cooperation
- Believes Great Student Involvement = Great Commitment

Today's students make the campus s________.

Answers: Scorekeeper, around. Guide, stronger.

Typical Responses from the 5 Management Types

1. ______________________ "What can you do to return to class on time after P.E.?"

2. ______________________ "You're late for class. Don't bother with the office. Just slip into your seat."

3. ______________________ "You were late last week, late yesterday and late today. You ought to be more responsible. You'll never have a recess or keep a job always being late."

4. ______________________ "I've had slow students before, but your body must be a petrified snail!"

5. ______________________ "That's a warning."

Answers: 1. Vision Manager 2. Permissive 3. Parental 4. Authoritarian 5. Monitor

Personal Enlightenment Hierarchy

By looking at the hierarchy below, determine your level of participation in your school's success. What could you change to become more involved in the success of your school?

Level of Participation	General Indicators
Antithetical	Exhibits anti-social behavior. Opposes personal and group vision and goals. Defiant: "I oppose whatever it is everyone else wants."
Noncompliant	Does not value the campus vision. Will not do what's expected. "You can't make me do it. My contract says I don't have to do that."
Apathetic	Neither for nor against vision (goals). Indifferent. "Can I go now? When will this meeting be over?" Does paperwork during meetings.
Grudging Accordance	Does not value the vision, but will comply to avoid negative consequences. "I'll do it, but I'll make it known that I don't support it."
Formal Accordance	Sees some value in the vision, but will only meet minimum standards. "I will do as you direct me, but no more, and keep my thoughts to myself."
Genuine Accordance	Sees value in the vision. Not only meets requests but enlists others to put forth quality effort. Exceeds standards. "I enjoy what I do and I share my enthusiasm with others."
Genuine Commitment	Wants to accomplish the vision everyday. Will complete the plan without further direction. "I am self-motivated and love what I do."
True Enlightenment	Will go beyond the vision. Passionately does whatever it takes to reach success. Revises & creates the strategies to do personal best. Inspires others to follow. "I am part of a quality team effort and I will help others."

- **How committed are you to the vision and goals of your school?**
- **How committed are you to your own goals and dreams?**
- **How committed can you expect your kids to be?**

**Your students can only be as committed as you are.
Do your students have quality role models
to help them to reach true enlightenment?**

"You Hold the Key"

Some kids see the world
in a very different way.
They really are not bad kids
just living a different way.

They hide their lack
behind actions often mean.
Sometime they're loud-rarely proud-
caught somewhere in-between.

Some don't try very hard-
they just don't seem to care.
What in heaven's name
is behind their hard, blank stare?

Whether sullen or rowdy
or too stubborn in every way,
These are the kids that are hard to reach
always getting in your way.

Yet, you signed-on to teach this year.
You're here to do your part.
A great man said "There's nothing stronger
than a loyal volunteer's heart!"

You come armed with books
and knowledge to share,
but without your love
they don't have a prayer.

Bring hope along, too,
for today that's what kids need.
So fill them with hope,
and your words they will heed.

Is it easy? Who said so?
They must have been wrong.
You've got to hang in there
with passion stay strong.

Commit to yourself
to inspire and enlighten.
You will reach that child-
their life you will brighten

And always remember
though the world may not see,
That kids are a locked treasure
and it's you who holds the key.

Rick Pehrson

There is no "I" in fear, but "I" is in the middle of "motivate." Ideally, it is the "I" that must initiate action. *Vision Management©* places the responsibility for motivation on the internal controls of the individual.

Using authoritarian power works because it makes youngsters fearful. Forced compliance is a hollow victory. When using Authoritarian, Parental, Permissive or Monitor communication, students do not learn to operate their internal controls.

The best motivation is self-motivation. A fellow says to me, "I wish someone would come by and turn me on." I answer, "What if they don't show up? You've got to have a better plan for your life."

Jim Rohn

Come On Let's Sift Again!

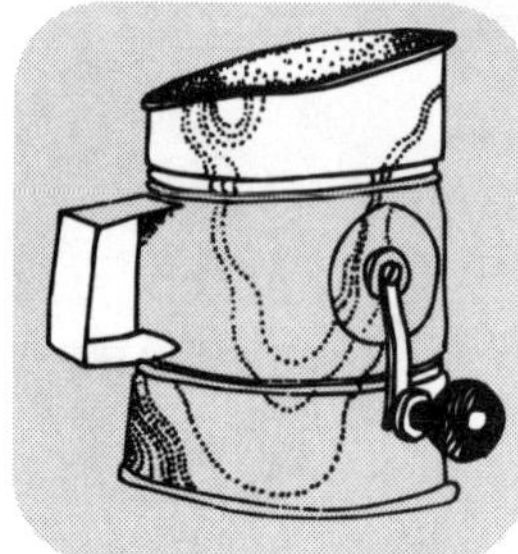

Awareness:

I want to be ________________.
(management style)

I tick-off ____________________.

My thoughts:

1. I believe I primarily operate in the ________________ management style.
2. My secondary style might be ____________________.
3. Who in my life do I "tick-off" with my communication style?
4. What outward signs of rejection have I been receiving?
5. Who "ticks me off"?
6. What bothers me about the person who "ticks me off"?
7. Do I ever do the same thing as the person who bothers me?
8. What am I going to do differently?

"No matter what Discipline Management system you use, it will only be as effective as your management style will allow."

Chapter 3

Take This Job And LOVE It!

Guiding the Student to Self-Management

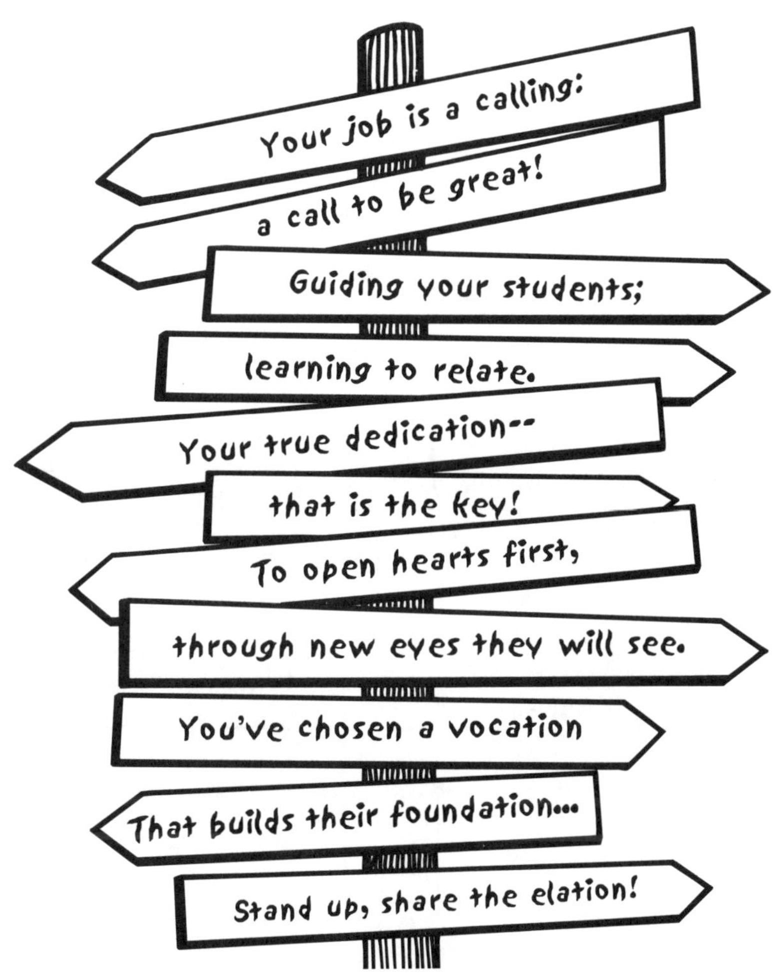

"Our challenge is to inspire all students to become their personal best."

THE PATH TO FOCUS YOUR THINKING

What do you hope will be the outcome of your efforts with students in your career?

Ask yourself, how much effort am I putting into my hoped-for outcome? Your students may mirror your energy, attitude, perseverance, and willingness to try new things.

List things you do with students the first day of the school year.

Students have reported to us that the most relevant thing a teacher can do is begin to build a positive relationship with them. Being warm & caring, laying out with excitement their curriculum and telling them what you believe in--primarily in them.

What do you think your students say when they get home about their first day of school?

85% say it was "boring."

What would most of your students say why they come to school?

Our research indicated that by third grade, students primarily said they come to school to see their friends. PK-K said to learn, 1st to learn to read, 2nd to learn to read better. 3rd-10th to see their friends. Eleventh-twelfth was because they had to.

The Path to Focus Your Thinking

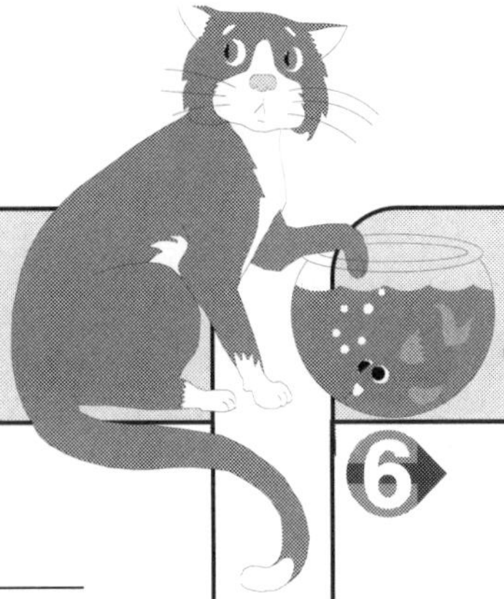

What is PRIDE?

5

Having Self-R____________

Having Self-E____________

Teaching students to have this is a primary goal of *Vision Management©*.

Before you can change students' ...

6

... a____________s,
you must change their
b____________s.

Most management programs punish students into compliance. We believe if you can change their outlook (belief), they willingly change unacceptable actions.

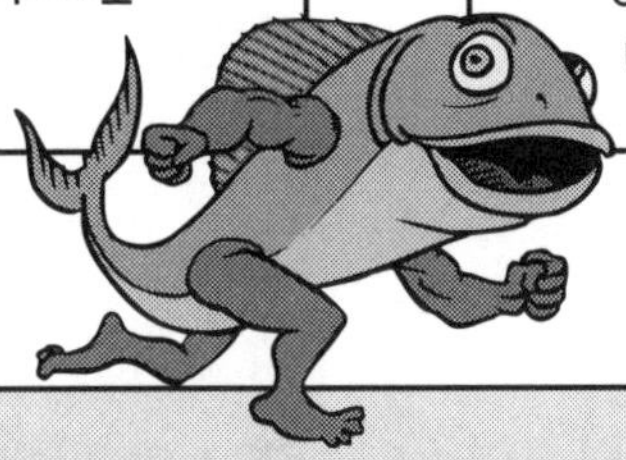

To kids the word "discipline," means ________________.

7

Discipline is an important v______.
It is the ability to stay f_______
while moving toward a g______.

Change their belief about the word, "discipline." Use a hand signal that means "get focused." Your students will prefer that to getting demerits or colors changed.

Answers: 5. Respect, Esteem 6. actions, beliefs 7. punishment, value, focused, goal

Guiding Students to Focus on Self-Improvement

A Key Word: "PRIDE"

The word **"pride"** is used frequently in *Vision Management's©* vocabulary and on portfolios to exemplify a high level of personal achievement accomplished by our students. Having increased their "pride" means that self-belief and self-respect are elevated to a point where students have begun to make sound, positive choices about their behavior and academic decisions.

To move them to a higher level of self-actualization that is vital for even greater success, it is necessary to rekindle that empowering moment of high self-belief. They must be motivated to determine their self-ideal. To accomplish this ask the question: **"What would they want, do or become if nothing could stop them?"** That answer becomes part of the students' self-ideal.

> *"What would they want to become if nothing could stop them?"*

Barriers exist in students' minds whose pride in their achievements has been dashed in non-supportive environments. They do not believe in themselves enough to have a motivating self-ideal. **We do not want our students to become adults who never reach their potential.** We do not want their confidence so low that they cease believing in themselves.

Too many students have given up entirely. Our educational system fails if we do not believe in them strongly enough to teach them how to "vision" their future, nor to teach them how to dream. Our calling is to show them how to make their dreams into goals, and to break goals into baby steps or action steps they can make, monitor and master. **By not creating "vision," we have taught self-limiting behavior. With "vision," dreams become reality.**

> *"By not creating 'vision,' we have taught self-limiting behavior."*

This chapter will deal with removing barriers to success. Your job is to stretch the mind of the child to have a "vision" of high achievement. Your students must be able to "see" themselves being successful. They must have the resilience to tear down walls and only build bridges to the gateways that lead to the achievement of their goals.

You will enjoy guiding your students to have focus on their education which is the key to their future. The following four steps are a natural and fun way to guide them down a path of "self-belief" and personal "pride." We've proven it can be done. Now you go out and do it, too!

4 Steps to Student Self-Improvement

Ask the following four questions to your students. Take four class periods or advisory sessions or more, if necessary, to do an interactive lesson with each question. It will be worth the time!

The quality of these lessons will be the foundation for your students' self-management and self-motivation skills. Therefore, do a good job! Create dynamic lessons using the following ideas. Allow time for collaboration. Create an activity where students can stand, move and THINK.

1 What's So Important About One's Education?

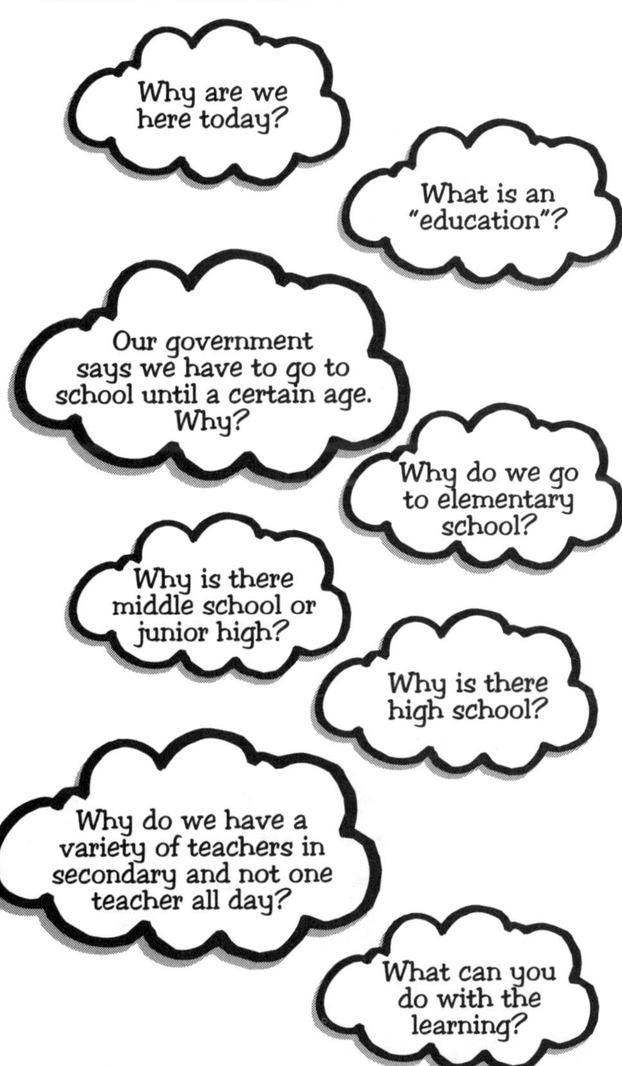

Getting the Best from Students

Kids need to be motivated to have a positive attitude--the first day, after holidays, and the beginning of a new grading period.

Ask them, **"Why are you here today?"** (THEY WRITE ANSWERS ON ONE PIECE OF BUTCHER PAPER OR ON THE BOARD.)

"You wrote many different reasons why you are here. Now answer this question: what is an education? (ALLOW THEM TO STRUGGLE.) **I am going to put you into groups of four. The person with the curliest hair gets: 1 dictionary, 1 piece of chart paper, 1 pencil, 1 set of markers, 1 sheet of paper for the group."**

"The person with the biggest hands looks up the word, 'education.' The person with the smallest hands writes the definition on the sheet of paper. Discuss what 'education' means. Collectively rewrite the definition in your own words."

"Look at what Will Rogers said about an education. 'Short-change your education now and you will be short of change the rest of your life.'" What does that mean? Discuss. (PUT ON BOARD OR OVERHEAD.)

"Now, as a team, you will create a soon-to-be-famous quotation about what the value of education means to you. It can be a rap, rhyme, story, song, saying or picture.

Once you have it the way you want, write it on the large poster and decorate it. Because it is quotation, what will it need to have? (QUOTATION MARKS.)

How will we know who wrote it? (THE AUTHORS ARE LISTED AT THE END.)

When completed each group sings, raps, tells or explains their poster.

Tip: Display in hallways, classroom walls or ceiling! Keep up for Parent Night.

Would You Like to Motivate & Inspire Your Students Daily?

I don't think kids know that they are supposed to have a positive attitude. I don't think some teachers know that either. Negative people need to be motivated and trained to have a positive attitude. That positivism must exist from the first day of class to the last day of the school year.

One helpful tool is "*Day2Day©* - 180 Inspirational and Motivational Messages." There is a message for each day of the school year. Following is a week's worth to get you started.

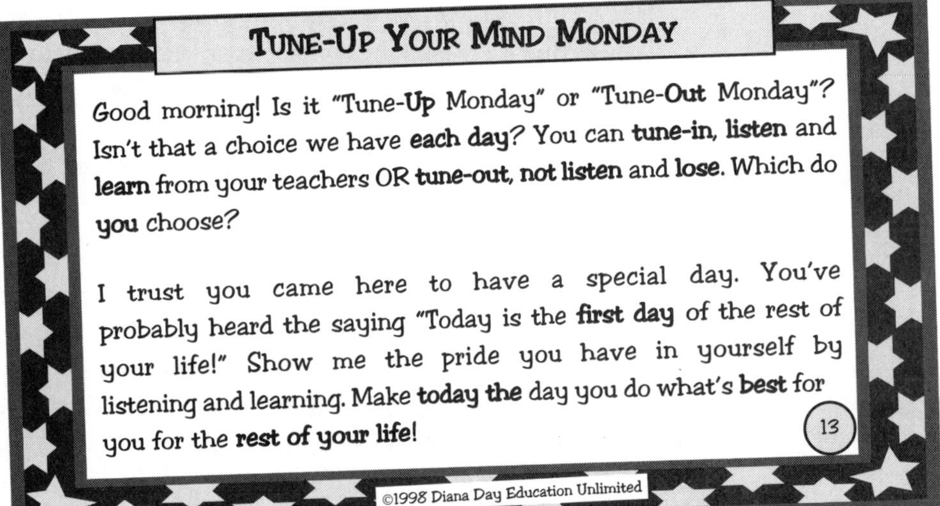

Tune-Up Your Mind Monday

Good morning! Is it "Tune-**Up** Monday" or "Tune-**Out** Monday"? Isn't that a choice we have **each day**? You can **tune-in**, **listen** and **learn** from your teachers OR **tune-out**, **not listen** and **lose**. Which do **you** choose?

I trust you came here to have a special day. You've probably heard the saying "Today is the **first day** of the rest of your life!" Show me the pride you have in yourself by listening and learning. Make **today the** day you do what's **best** for you for the **rest of your life**!

13

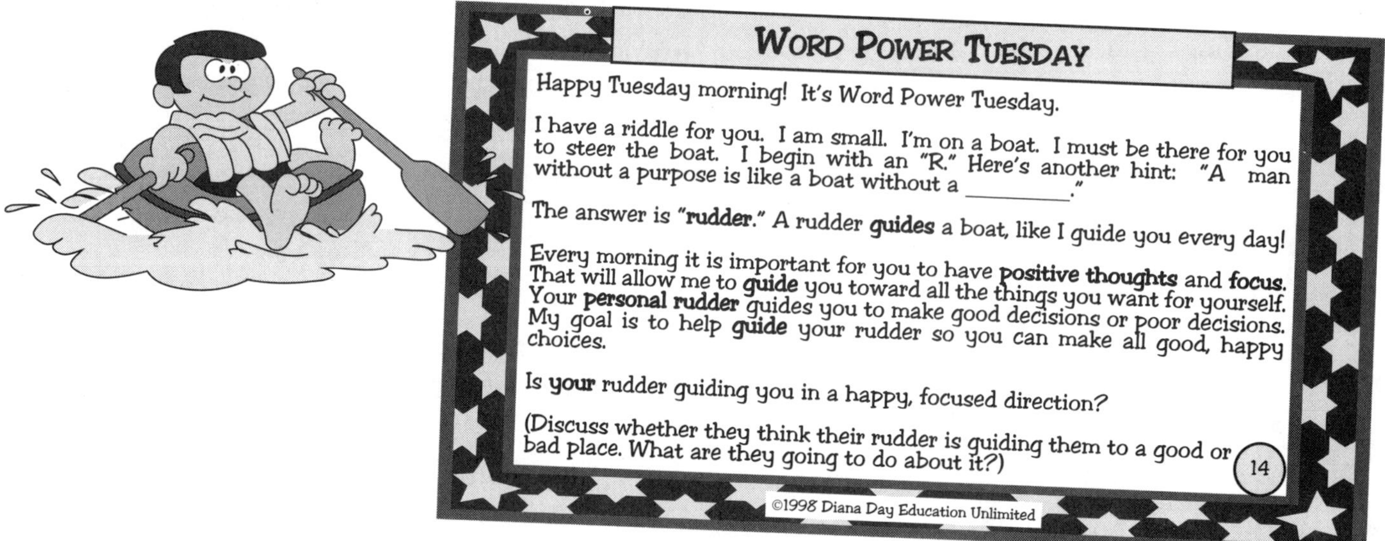

Word Power Tuesday

Happy Tuesday morning! It's Word Power Tuesday.

I have a riddle for you. I am small. I'm on a boat. I must be there for you to steer the boat. I begin with an "R." Here's another hint: "A man without a purpose is like a boat without a _________."

The answer is "**rudder.**" A rudder **guides** a boat, like I guide you every day!

Every morning it is important for you to have **positive thoughts** and **focus.** That will allow me to **guide** you toward all the things you want for yourself. Your **personal rudder** guides you to make good decisions or poor decisions. My goal is to help **guide** your rudder so you can make all good, happy choices.

Is **your** rudder guiding you in a happy, focused direction?

(Discuss whether they think their rudder is guiding them to a good or bad place. What are they going to do about it?)

14

For more about *Day2Day©* - see page 137.

WOULD YOU LIKE TO REFOCUS YOUR CAMPUS DAILY?

WIN-WIN WEDNESDAY

A Warm Wednesday Welcome to each of you.

Please listen silently. **Point to** the person who knows more than anyone in your room. (pause) **Smile at** the person who wants you to succeed in your life. (pause) **Nod your head** if you plan to cooperate and learn as much as you can this year.

I want to make a difference in your lives. Sometimes teachers do not find out if they have made a difference in their students' lives.

Our quotation today is : "Teachers affect eternity. They never know where their contribution stops." ...Diana Day

What is eternity? How long is eternity? Let's discuss this. Which teacher contributed to your life and how? You will see that a teacher's influence or contribution will be with you for your lifetime.

Students, be proud of our wonderful teachers who care so deeply about you.

15

AWESOME ATTITUDE THURSDAY

Happy Thursday Morning! It's Awesome Attitude Thursday!

Have you noticed how much more **polite** students are compared to last year? Other teachers have told me you are much **kinder** this year, too.

I remember last year asking two students to pick up some paper in the hall. One said, "It's not **my** paper." The other said, "Why do I have to pick up everyone else's mess?" Can you imagine saying **that** to an adult who has **politely** asked you to do something? These students had **no** self-pride. They weren't unhappy about picking up paper, they were unhappy with themselves. How they acted has a name. It's called: **RUDE.**

Think about this: "It is not your **IQ** that makes you a good person, it's your **I-WILL** that counts." ...Diana Day

For a week, let's practice "**I WILL**" to every request an adult in this school gives you. Let's notice the difference on our campus.

Practice **I-WILLINGNESS! Not rudeness!**

16

FOCUS FRIDAY

Happy, happy Friday! Fridays deserve two "happys" in front of them! This is Focus Friday where we look back at our week and refocus for the next week.

Our quotation for the day is: "**Shortchange** your education now and you may be **short of change** the rest of your life." What does that mean?

Are you giving 100% to your education, or are you fooling around and not caring about learning? What will happen to people who shortchange themselves during their school years? Are you allowing me to help you?

Today write what could happen to you if you don't have pride in your work, your home, your **teachers**, your **school**, or in **yourself**. What would you become? Is that what you want? Yes or no?

Have PRIDE! Believe 100% in **yourself**!

17

4 Steps to Student Self-Improvement

"You know me as a coach, science, math, fourth grade teacher. You don't know me as a person. Let me tell you about the moment that I decided to be a teacher."

Your thoughts:

Why Should I Listen to My Teacher?

Why I became a teacher.

The teacher who inspired me to become a teacher.

The event that motivated me to become a teacher.

Why I chose to become a __________ teacher.

3 WHY DO I HAVE TO LEARN THIS?

Give a commercial about what wonderful things they will learn during the semester.

Why what I teach is of value to you.

Share the focus or purpose of your teaching.

A commercial is vital at this step! They will not be able to write a goal for your class if they do not know what they will be expected to learn. **Have great enthusiasm while giving a preview of your subject matter.** Remember, do not get preachy. Ask questions to get enthusiasm high so they will want to learn what you will be sharing!

4 IS ANYONE OUT THERE LISTENING?

Say: "I feel so strongly about what you will be learning that I have written a promise to you, and have signed it." It is called my "PEDS." Do you know what that means? (*Professional Educator Dedication Statement.)*

Show them the "PEDS" you have written especially for them.

Discuss your commitment to them.

Have students write an SDS (Student Dedication Statement). See page 42 .

MY COMMERCIAL:

VALUE OF MY CLASS TO THEM:

How to Write a PEDS

For generations, to respect the authority of educators and parents was a given. Today, many of our students, along with their parents, are disrespectful and discourteous. Some educators and authority figures are also discourteous. It seems some folks expect the worst, are defensive, and unwilling to have forgiveness.

Let your dedication to your students be known to parents and students alike. Set the tone for courtesy, civility and communication by posting your PEDS on your door. Sign it. Remind students of your PEDS when they think the worst.

The Outcomes of Writing Your PEDS

1. Student understands why the teacher feels so strongly about students getting an education.

2. It allows students to ask questions of teachers that typically do not get asked. This improves communication, builds trust and initiates a good relationship between teacher and students.

3. It demonstrates the teacher's sincerity and awareness of students' needs, achievement and anticipated success.

The Goal of Writing Your PEDS

"To commit to writing why you became a teacher or what your professional aspirations are for both your students and you."

Guidelines for Writing an Effective PEDS

To be effective the PEDS would be:

- *Simple* (Language that your grade level can read or understand)
- C-O-N-C-I-S-E (25 words or less)
- Decisive (Reminds us to take action)!!!
- Motivational (Stirs emotion for both reader and writer)

A Worksheet to Create Your PEDS

Write your name, grade level or subject matter in a vertical line. Think of a positive characteristic or value you believe in and want to dedicate to your students. It can start with the beginning letter of that line.

Why did you choose to become an educator?

Was there an event that inspired you to become an educator?

What is a "model educator"?

Why did you choose your grade level or subject?

What do you want your students to accomplish this year?

What is your dedication to accomplish your professional goals?

Professional Educator Dedication Statement

Our PEDS empowers us to become the best each of us can be according to our own standard of evaluation. Our PEDS is also a statement about persistence. When your persistence is greater than your students' resistance, you will prevail. In other words, your vision is greater than theirs.

Professional Educator Dedication Statements

Great will be my attitude
Opening minds to a love for learning
Always respecting the needs of others
Loving and nurturing at all times
Success of my students is my reward

Learn to be fair & responsible to others
Eager & willing to learn
Achieve your goals in life
Respect others as you wish to be respected
Never say you can't; say I can

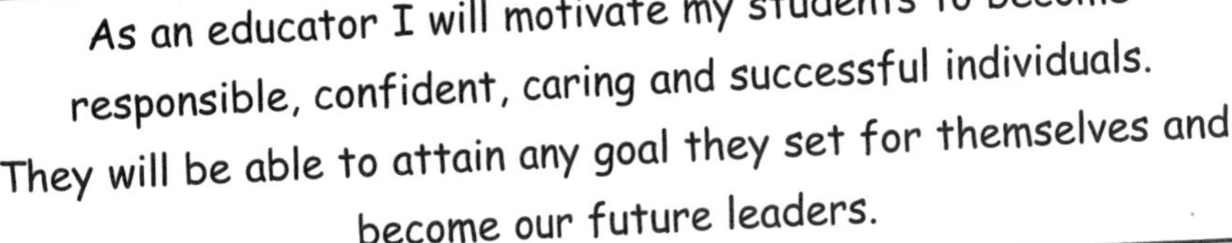

As an educator I will motivate my students to become responsible, confident, caring and successful individuals. They will be able to attain any goal they set for themselves and become our future leaders.

Caring is the key
Open to new ideas
Uplifting people is my job
Never give up
Self-Esteem is taught daily
Empathetic educator
Live one day at a time
Organization is a must
Regard for all

The Challenge To Excel

I will--
Make learning fun
Appreciate my student's differences
Guide my students down a positive path
Instill in my students a desire for knowledge and responsibility
Contribute to my students everyday a part of me through respect, love, kindness and fairness

I'VE STUDIED FOR YEARS--SIXTEEN OR MORE.
I'VE INFO TO SHARE WITH MORE LEARNING IN STORE.
YOU KNOW ABOUT YOUTH; I KNOW ABOUT LIFE.
YOU KNOW ABOUT FREEDOM; I KNOW ABOUT STRIFE.
YOU'RE LIVING THE POWER OF TRIUMPHANT YOUTH.
WE ALL SEARCH FOR PLEASURE, FOR ANSWERS, FOR TRUTH.
WE CAN WALK TOGETHER-- AND TALK ON THE WAY.
IF EITHER WILL LISTEN, IT WILL BE A GREAT DAY.

"From a Teacher" by Linda Jessie-Jones

Professional Educator Dedication Statements

Today influences tomorrow
Everyone should feel safe and secure
Allow learning through success and mistakes
Class will "run" when learning is fun
Hear every student
Encourage curiosity
Remember, we all have special gifts

We care when you are here.
We care when you are not here-
you are missed!
Each student counts to us
in the Attendance Office.

I want to instill in my students
the desire to learn by being:

Positive and persistent
On top of things
Sensitive toward their feelings
Inspirational
Totally committed
In every form and way
Voice and ears of children
Excellent provider of the mind

Supportive
Teachers
Understand
Differences;
Ensure
Numerous
Teaching
Strategies

My attitude is the key
I am the example
Success and no less
Stay calm and consistent
I achieve what I believe
Open eyes, ears and mind
Never give up

LISTEN TO THEIR NEEDS
EDUCATE EFFECTIVELY
ACHIEVE GOALS
REACH HIGHEST POTENTIAL
NEVER GIVE UP

I dedicate my time and talents to making a positive change in each of my students. **I will** make my classroom a structured and loving haven for the learning of academics and self-respect. **I believe** that each child is unique and each day **I will** teach my students to make responsible choices which will lead them to success.

Professional Educator Dedication Statements

Enrich minds
Develop their verbal, mental, social, emotional and physical skills
Utilize and accommodate the various learning styles
Commit to the success of all students
Allow them to make mistakes
Teach them to be respectful, responsible and caring
Open minds to be creative and self-confident
Respect them as I would want to be respected

My Vision is to be:

- An understanding and caring person
- To set high standards for myself as well as my students
- To help each student to achieve their goals
- To listen and act with a caring spirit that reflects love, kindness, gentleness, goodness, patience and joy.

Rhonda Smith is my name
Teaching is my game.

Having you in school
shows that you're pretty cool.

For you know the trick
To reading, writing and arithmetic.

You are nobody's fool
That's because you can follow the school's rule.

I know that you are the best
So let's show everyone all those high scores on the TAAS test.

Come on-stay cool-learn and stretch your mind
After all you're one of a kind!

I want to be a teacher who:

Transmits to students a desire for knowledge
Expects each student to succeed
Allows students to take risks
Communicates with parents and peers
Has a safe and nurturing classroom
Enables students to reach their potential
Smiles!

Thanks to the great teachers at:
Comfort High School, Comfort, Texas
Crockett Elementary, Harlingen, Texas
Lincoln Elementary School, Fort Madison, Iowa
Levi Fry Intermediate School, Texas City, Texas
St. Louis High School, Honolulu, Hawaii
Bellaire Elementary, Deer Valley, Arizona
Hominy Public Schools, Oklahoma

Goes into Pride Folder.

Write your name here → _______________'s Dedication to Getting An Education

Write your promise to yourself on the t-shirt and then decorate it.

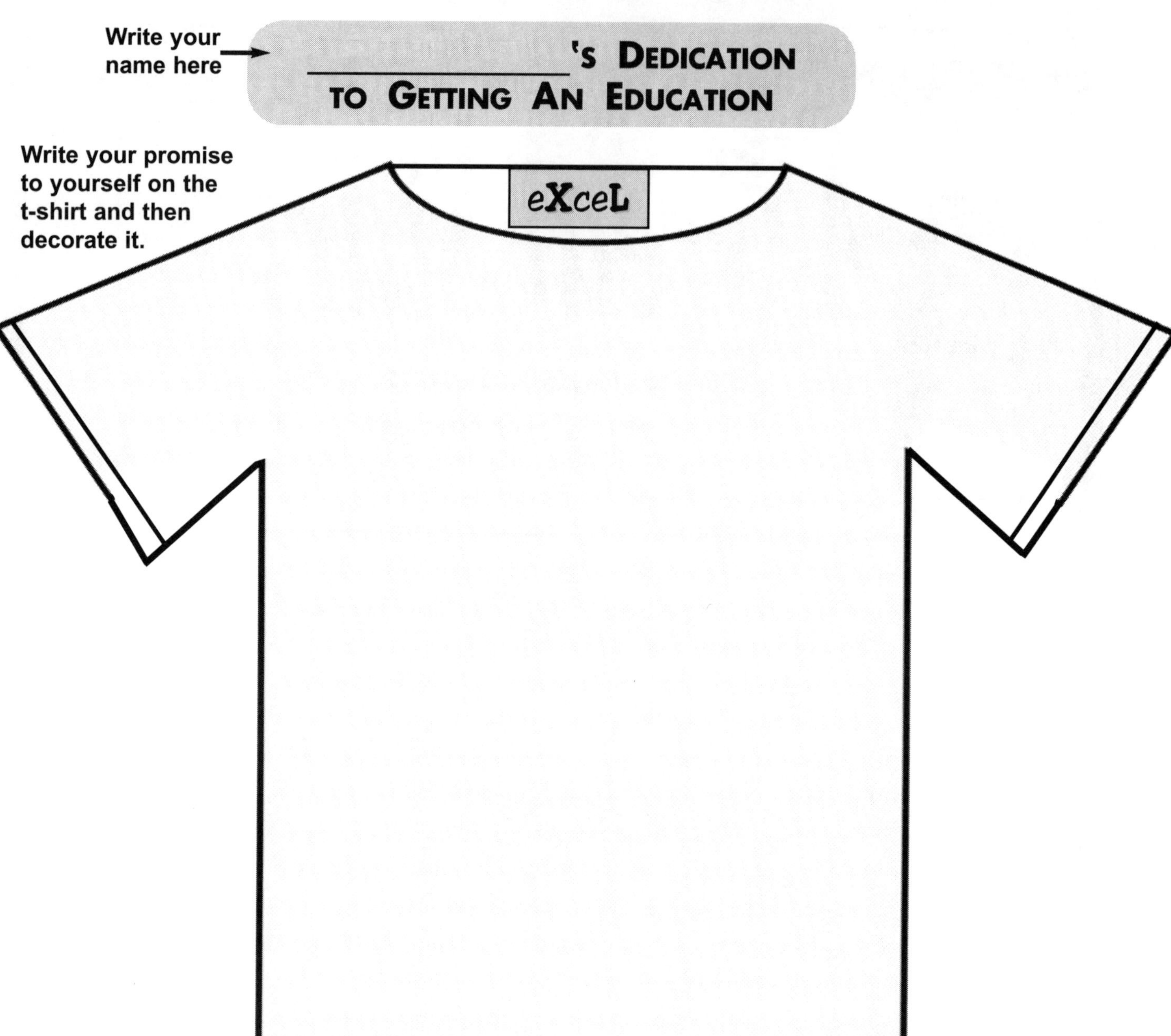

People Who Believe in Me *(Family, teachers, friends)*

Name	Date	Comment
1. ______	______	______
2. ______	______	______
3. ______	______	______
4. ______	______	______
5. ______	______	______

Chapter 4

Goal-For-It!

Creating Student Self-Determination

"A journey of a thousand miles begins with a single step."

Make Your Dreams Come True: Goal Targeting

We used to call them New Year's Resolutions. They are made and broken by Valentine's Day. We don't know how to make them, let alone how to keep them. We just know that we want to change our lives.

Change-conscious authors of the 90's, wanting us to alter our habits, changed "resolutions" to "goals," and now we are learning how to set them all year long. The pity is that we set 'em and forget 'em.

A goal is a promise to action. Mental goal setting doesn't mean that you will reach your goals. **You must write them down.**

A study conducted by Harvard University showed that the top 3% of the graduating class were systematic **writers** of goals. A follow-up study thirty years later in l986, showed this group were significantly more successful than the rest of the class. The primary difference was they were still **writing goals--targeting action.**

Want to Know How Successful People Accomplish Their Goals?

First, is that successful people **write** their goals as soon as they think of something they want to achieve. They do not just hope for what they want; they, steadfastly, write out *exactly* what they want. They write in great **detail!** Is your goal so clear in your mind that you could write it in detail?

Albert Einstein wrote that there have been no great people in the world since we stopped writing journals for personal reflection. Do we take time to reflect upon what we have accomplished and what we want to do next?

Writing goals crystallizes your thinking. It takes your wants from the recesses of your mind to reality on paper. Otherwise, your goals are mere flashes of your imagination!

Second, goal-targeters write goals so **clearly,** and in such **detail,** that they can see themselves achieving that goal. They see themselves smiling when being handed a paper with a good grade, getting an award, throwing a touchdown, making a basket, having friends, getting a great job. This is called **"visualization." What do you see yourself accomplishing?**

Third, goal-targeters write their goals in a way that sounds like it has happened. (I make B's in science.) That's called writing them in the **"positive."** You wouldn't write what you don't want to happen. ("I don't want to make a bad grade in science.") That's writing in the "negative."

Remember, you want your brain to **visualize** your goal. What would your mind see if you wrote "I don't want to make a bad grade in science"? (Probably a "D" or "F" on a paper!) **Can you think of a way to say your goal in the positive?** ("I make 'A's.' I studied so much, I made an 'A.'")

MAKE YOUR DREAMS COME TRUE: GOAL TARGETING

Fourth, goal targeters keep their lives in **balance** by setting goals in the most important areas of their lives: family, professional, spiritual, financial, social, mental and physical. **Write your goals in each of these key areas.**

Fifth, goal targeters divide their goals into **manageable time frames.** You can manage a five-year, annual, quarterly, and daily plans. Revise the timing, any time, without fear of failure. Break these goals into achievable action steps. Then, enter the steps of the action plan into your daily organizer. **What is your time frame for success?**

Sixth, it's important to celebrate each successful step of the journey. Don't wait until total achievement of your goal of a "B" in science. Celebrate each "B" you make. Tell yourself how great you are to have stuck with your study schedule. Give yourself a pat-on-the-back even if no one else does. Remember, you are now pleasing yourself. It's YOUR goal. What are your mini-achievements? **How will you celebrate in mini-ways?**

Seventh, should you make a "C," or even a "D," don't get down on yourself. No one climbs straight up a

> *"No one climbs straight up a mountain."*

mountain. They zigzag and even go down a bit before going back up. That's O.K. Thomas Edison had 10,000 experiments fail before he finally created electricity. When asked how he was able to keep his spirits up, he said, "I now know 10,000 ways not to make electricity!" **Have you ever gotten discouraged and given up on something you wanted? What would you now do differently?**

> *"Remember, your subconscious must believe you have a 50% chance of success to engage in the goal accomplishment process."*

Seven Tips to Write Meaningful Goals

"Target goals from the power of your own dreams"

1. Regularly write and review your goals.
2. Make your goals specific.
3. State your goals positively.
4. Remember to write goals for all areas of your life.
5. Put your goals into a reasonable time frame.
6. Believe in your ability to succeed.
7. Never, never give up!

Want Great Ideas to Teach Goal Writing?

Purpose of Goals

The purpose of goals is to focus your mental attention. The mind will not reach toward achievement until it has clear objectives. The magic begins when you **write your goals**. It is then that the switch is turned on, and the current begins to flow. The power to accomplish begins in earnest.

Power of Goals

- Is a promise to yourself
- Is something you want, or a focus upon what you want to become
- Does not harm or hurt you or other people
- Successful people rewrite their goals daily to increase focus

For Primary:

- Use *Goal-For-It!*© (K-4) to help students understand your discipline plan & learn how to write goals
- Ask students what goals they want to achieve
- List 2-3 goals on a wall chart, having students rate progress daily
- Evaluate progress on a graph
- Discuss ways to improve results and call these "action steps"

For Intermediate Grades:

- Students create PRIDE folders with PEDS & SDS attached to inside covers
- Students enjoy creating an acrostic of their name for their SDS
- Use *Goal-For-It!*© (5-12) to help students apply your management system and learn to goal set
- Students plot individual progress on PACE form
- Problem-solving occurs when students seek ways to improve personal scores on the PACE form

For Secondary:

- Focus on career goals & personal responsibility
- Use PACE form to achieve personal & academic goals
- Study 7-Step Goal-Targeting Process
- Use *Goal-For-It*© (5-12) to teach self-motivation, goal-targeting to graduate and get a job
- Use an organizer or student planner to store goal sheets. The planner is also their hall pass
- Set class goals on cooperative projects and assess progress

STUDENT GOAL WORKSHEET

GOALS
"One Step at a Time"

Name: ______________________________

Date: ______________________________

1. What do you want to accomplish in this class?
(What grade, skill, concept, ability, behavior?)

My goal is to: ______________________________

____

____

____

2. What action will you take to reach your goal?

1) ______________________________

2) ______________________________

3) ______________________________

4) ______________________________

5) ______________________________

3. What actions would take you away from your goal?

1) ______________________________

2) ______________________________

3) ______________________________

4) ______________________________

5) ______________________________

4. I will start working toward my goal ____________________.

5. If I am not successful at first, I will t _ _ again and n _ _ _ _, n_ _ _ _ give up.

____
Signature

My ***Learning Goal*** is: ______________________________

____

____

My Ladder of Success

My Learning Goal

My Behavior Goal

My Personal Goal

I will do the following to make it happen:

1. ______________________________
2. ______________________________
3. ______________________________

My ***Behavior Goal*** is: ______________________________

____

____

I will do the following to make it happen:

1. ______________________________
2. ______________________________
3. ______________________________

My ***Personal Goal*** is: ______________________________

____

____

I will do the following to make it happen:

1. ______________________________
2. ______________________________
3. ______________________________

______________________________ MY SIGNATURE

______________ DATE

YOUR NAME

Goal Sheet

2nd Quarter

My Learning Goal

Having looked at my grades, my goal for this quarter is: ______________

Action steps I will take to reach my goal:

1. ______________
2. ______________
3. ______________

What actions are taking me away from my goal?

1. ______________
2. ______________
3. ______________

My Behavior Goal

Having looked at my conduct & friendships, my goal for this quarter is:

Action steps I will take to reach my goal:

1. ______________
2. ______________
3. ______________

What actions are taking me away from my goal?

1. ______________
2. ______________
3. ______________

MY SIGNATURE

DATE

Goal Sheet

YOUR NAME _______________

3rd QUARTER

CHECK ONE: ❑ I am pleased with my progress! ❑ I need to focus more on my action steps.

CIRCLE ONE: Which do I need to focus upon this quarter?

My learning? My friendships/behavior?

ACTION!

1. What do I want to accomplish in this class?

   (What grade, skill, concept, ability, behavior?)

   My goal is to: ____

   ____

2. What action steps will I take to reach my goal?

   1.) ____

   2.) ____

   3.) ____

3. What actions are taking me away from my goal?

   1.) ____

   2.) ____

   3.) ____

4. When will I start working toward my goal? _______________________________.

5. What if I feel like giving up?
   If I am not successful at first, I will t _ _ again and n _ _ _ _, n _ _ _ _ give up.

What is keeping me from being successful? ____

____

_______________________________ MY SIGNATURE

_______________ DATE

www.dianaday.com • 972-278-7773

Home Stretch Goal Sheet

4TH QUARTER

YOUR NAME

What will make the biggest difference to help you reach success? ____________________

____

1. My ***Learning Goal*** is: ____

____

____

2. What action steps will I take to reach my goal?
   1.) ____
   2.) ____
   3.) ____
   4.) ____
   5.) ____

3. What actions are taking me away from my goal?
   1.) ____
   2.) ____
   3.) ____
   4.) ____
   5.) ____

THIN ICE

4. I will start working toward my goal ______________________.

5. If I am not successful at first, I will t _ _ again and n _ _ _ _, n_ _ _ _ give up.

I can do it!

By following my action steps, **I can succeed.**

______________________________ MY SIGNATURE

______________ DATE

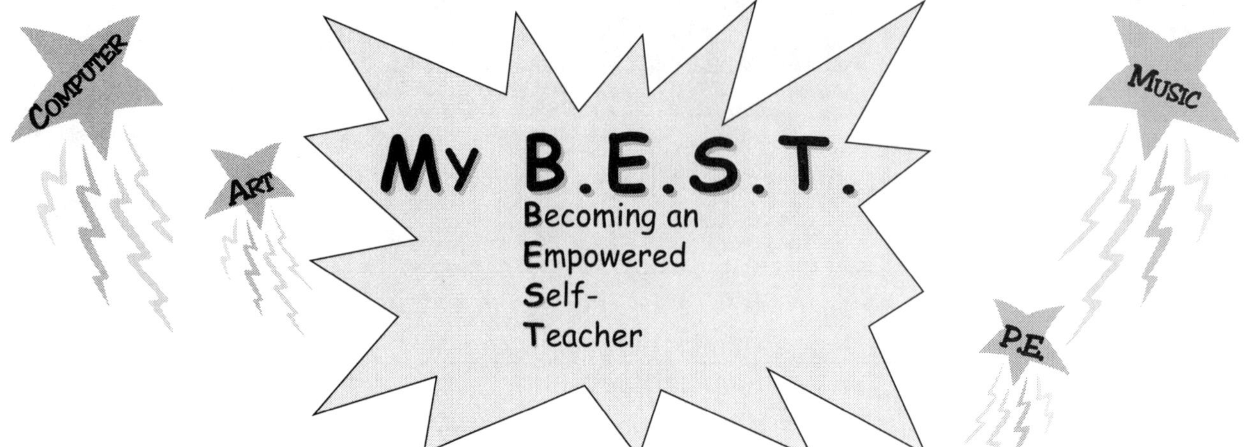

Name: ______________________________

My goal statement is:

I can accomplish my goal by following these action steps:

1. ______________________________
2. ______________________________
3. ______________________________
4. ______________________________
5. ______________________________

Professional Educator Dedication Statement

I commit to help you by:

____

____

____

____

____

____

How I'm Doing & How It Feels

Directions: By now you may be seeing a difference in your life because you are focusing on your goal.
If you feel you are successful, write about how you're doing, and how it feels.

OR

If you are not being successful, it may not be your goal but your action steps.
Look at your action steps to be sure: (1) they are helping you (2) you are following them.
If you need to change your action steps, commit to it now.
Write about how you are doing, and what you will do differently. If you feel you are not successful, write about how you're doing, how it feels and what you will do differently.

To The Top!

Name______________________________

Date ______________________________

FINISH

Getting Back on Track

Name ______________________ Date __________

1. Did you reach your goal? ________ Why or why not?

____

____

____

2. What do you want to do to get back on track? ______________________

____

____

3. What is the first step you will take to get refocused? ________________

____

____

4. Please rewrite the action steps you plan to take to get on target.

   1.)____

   2.)____

   3.)____

   4.)____

5. Is there anyone you would like to work with so you could be more successful? __________

   ____

   Who? ____

   How? ____

6. Would you like a private conference with me so we could just talk? ____________

   When is best for you? ______________________________

   Where could we do this?______________________________

Spiral Up or Spiral Down?

Do you think about a time when you really messed up?
Starting at #1, name each thing you did that caused the process.
Tell in detail.

Think about a time when you were awesome, did your best and things went right. Starting at #1, name each thing you did that made things go right.

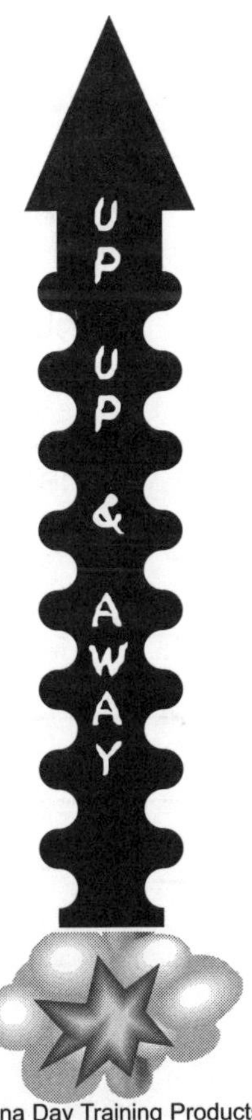

WANT MORE FRIENDS? LIVE BY TPS!

Today you will learn a word that you must live by each and every day of your life. Look up this word in the dictionary:

"INTEGRITY" means...________________________________

____

____

When you have integrity, your friendships will multiply!

3 WAYS TO HAVE INTEGRITY and MORE FRIENDS:

1 T Be Truthful	2 P Keep Promises	3 S Make Special
When you <u>always tell the truth</u>, people trust you.	When you <u>do what you say you will do</u>, people respect you.	When you <u>make others feel special</u>, people like you.
What is something you need to tell the truth about?	What do you need to do that you promised? Who will respect you?	What can you do to make someone feel special? Write in detail what you'd do.
______________________ ______________________ ______________________ ______________________ ______________________	______________________ ______________________ ______________________ ______________________ ______________________	______________________ ______________________ ______________________ ______________________ ______________________

Complete on other side, if needed.

www.dianaday.com • 972-278-7773

THE SIX HABITS OF SUCCESSFUL STUDENTS

1. **DETERMINE YOUR NEGATIVE HABITS.**
   I'm not pleased that I ... ______
   ____
   ____

2. **COMMIT TO CHANGE.**
   I promise to... ______________
   ____
   ____

3. **VISUALIZE NEW OUTCOMES.**
   I see myself... ______________
   ____
   ____

4. **HAVE CONFIDENCE IN YOUR ABILITY.**
   Now I will... ______________
   ____
   ____

5. **NEVER STOP YOUR NEW HABIT.**
   When I get off-track I need to...
   ____
   ____
   ____
   ____
   ____
   ____

6. **ALWAYS DO THE RIGHT THING FOR YOURSELF AND OTHERS.**
   Recently I made a good decision because I...______________
   ____
   ____
   ____
   ____
   ____

THE 4-D SOLUTION

By following your "4-D Solution," you will become more successful. Focus on your goals. Whenever you need to make a decision, use your 4-D's to help you DO THE RIGHT THING. You have four ways to handle a decision!

Dump It - "This is not good for me."
Be firm and strong about your decision.

What Do You Need to Dump?

Deliberate On It - This means give what someone wants you to do very careful thought and then make a decision.

What Do You Very Carefully Need to Think About?

Desire It - Want success so badly that you can visualize yourself having or getting all that you want.

What Do You Desire?

Do It - Always say to yourself, "Do it now...Do it now...Do it now."

Name Several Things That You Need To Do Now.

List every reason you can think of to not be here and to be back in your classroom.

10.

9.

8.

7.

6.

5.

4.

3.

2.

3...2...1...Blastoff!

Three things I have learned from being in a Refocus Area:

1.
2.
3.

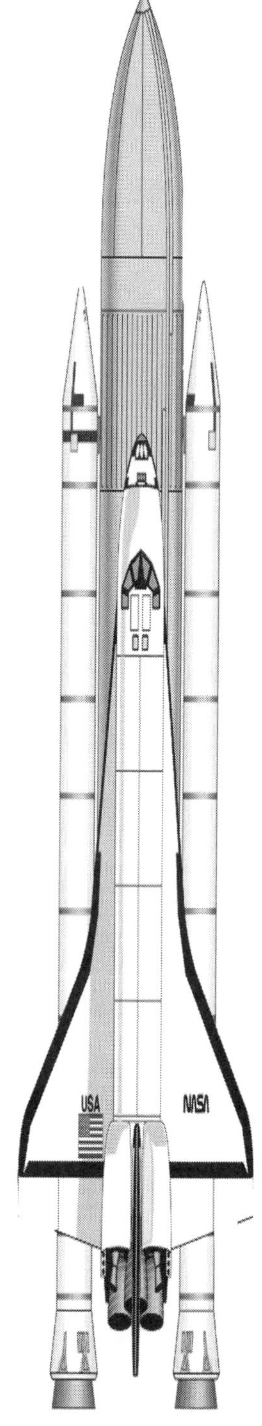

Tomorrow I will do the following differently:

1.
2.
3.

These people can help me by doing this:

1.
2.
3.

A FEATHER IN YOUR CAPS

Diana hears that the most difficult thing to do after the training session is to implement the many ideas presented by her and audience members. When many valid ideas are presented, it seems impossible to take action upon each one immediately.

This form will help you break the barriers of inertia, seemingly unsurmountable challenges, or time restrictions. **The key to achievement is to focus upon the most important idea presented and to act upon it immediately.**

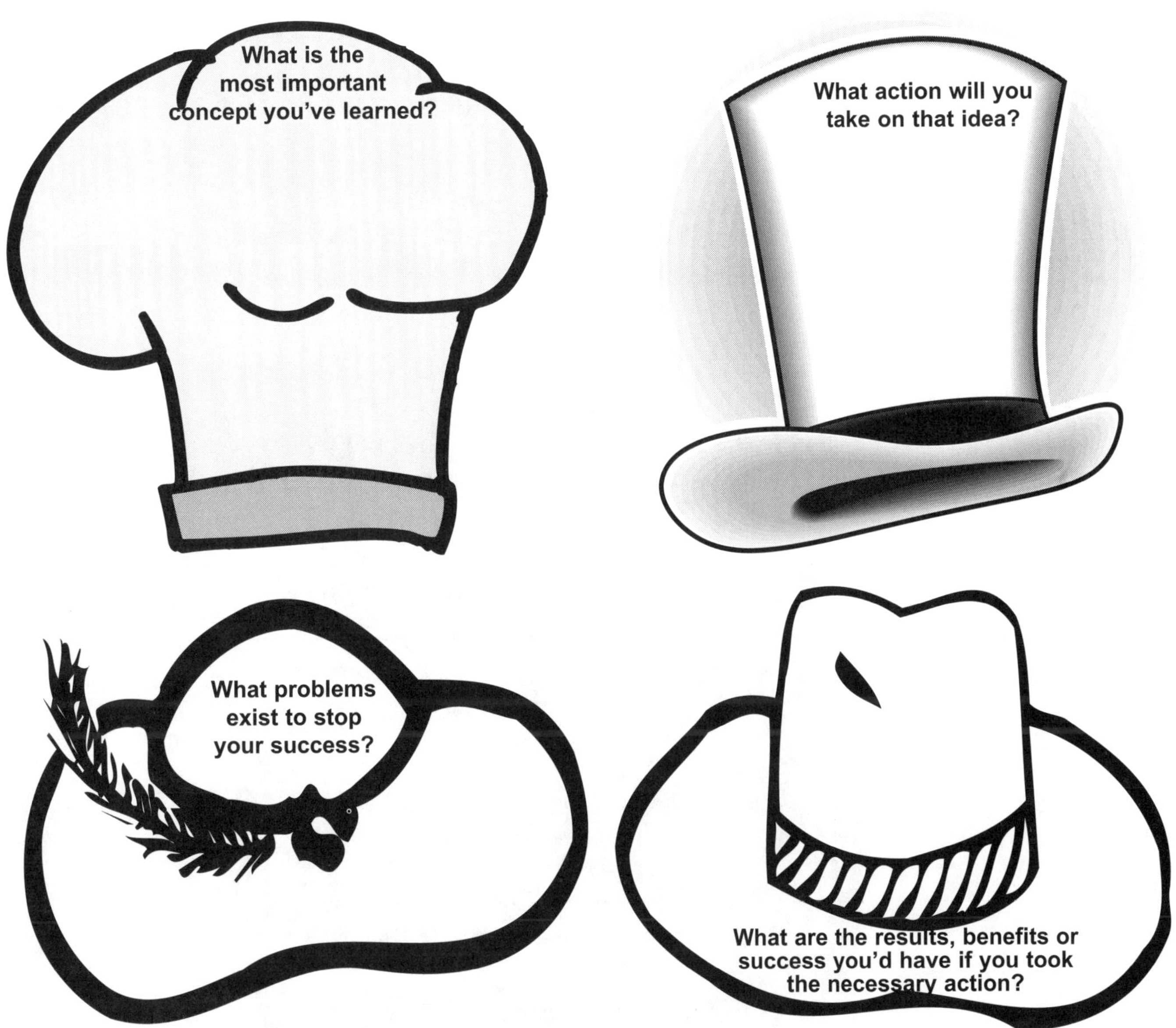

Promise yourself to take action upon what you have learned.
I will take action by ___________ (date) .

____
Signed

Put Yourself in the Driver's Seat

1. Your headlights give you vision. Where do you want to go?
2. Who is the driver?
3. Is anyone else involved?
4. What do you need to take with you to go where you want to go?
5. What can you do to become self-motivated? How can you fuel yourself to do the right thing?
6. Speed: How quickly do you want to go?
7. What do you need to get rid of to get where you want to go?

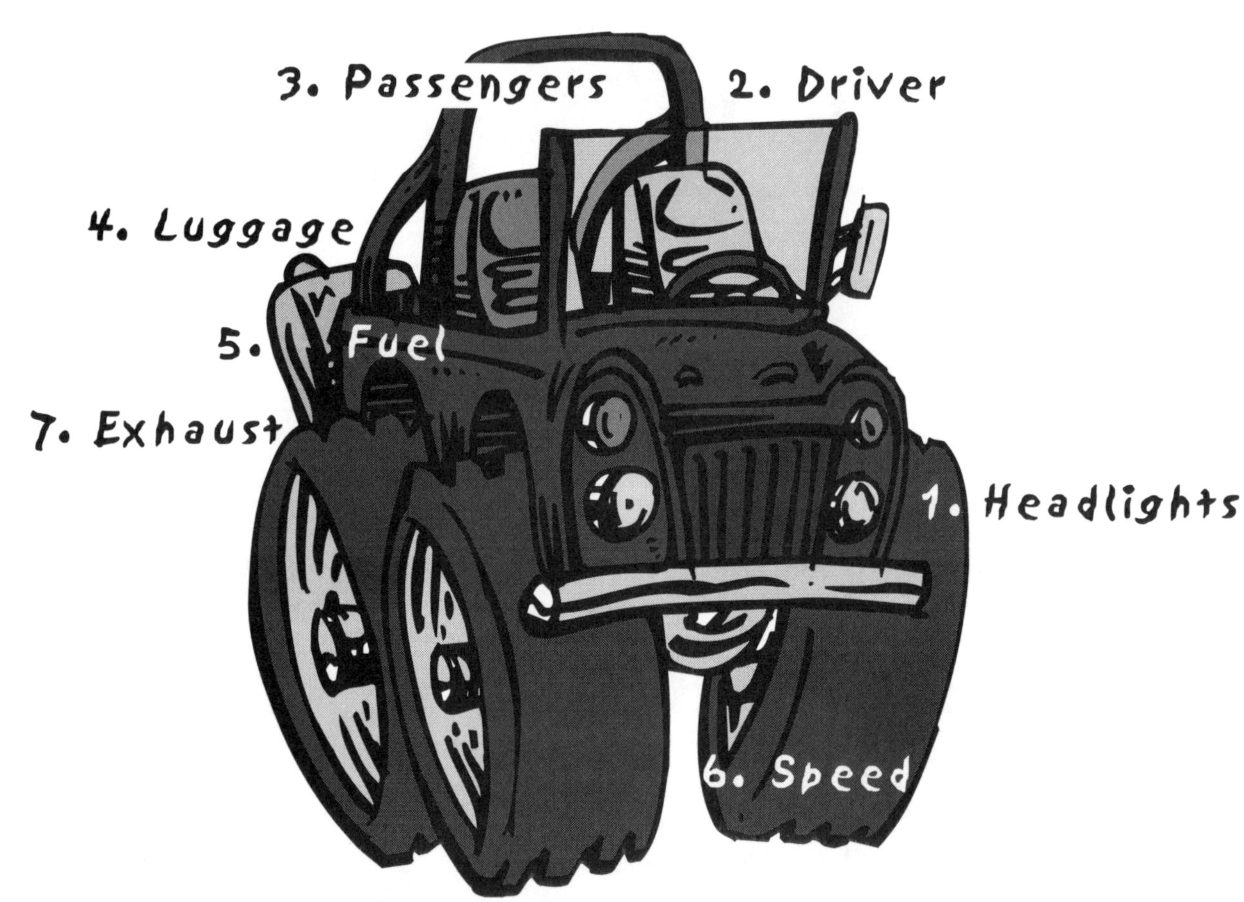

www.dianaday.com • 972-278-7773

WHAT'S THE CORNERSTONE OF YOUR BEHAVIOR MANAGEMENT SYSTEM?

The P_______ F_______ is the cornerstone of your student/teacher problem-solving sessions, meetings with the counselor, on-site parent conferences, and office referrals.

In each of these meetings, the student is asked to verbally review his goal with the adult leading the session. Inquire about his progress toward reaching his goals. Action steps can be discussed and always ask if his actions are helping or hurting him to successfully reach those goals. This session is meant to be helpful with kind conversation, always encouraging the student to follow the steps he set forth to reach his goal.

Many times the student may enter the meeting with a goal that is not totally relevant to the problem at-hand. He can be encouraged to create another goal sheet with a more pressing goal and action steps that will begin to solve the problem he's gotten himself into.

Focusing upon the student's goal, makes this meeting non-confrontational and aimed at achievement--not focused on shame, guilt, or past mistakes. Every adult's goal is to get the student to refocus back to his primary purpose in school…HIS goal.

Kids have lost their sense of self.
They are looking for value outside themselves (gangs, acting out behaviors, etc.).
PRIDE folders prove to students that they have a large inventory of ability (value) that will be reinforced once they take responsibility for their learning. Some student's high degree of damaging, acting-out behavior is often a distraction from greater pain.
This is covered in the *Challenging Students*© workshop.

1. G_______ Sheets
2. Professional Educator D_____________ Statement
3. S______________ Dedication Statement
4. C______________-Building Worksheets
5. A______________, certificates or positive teacher notes
6. P__________ the student is proud of
7. Letter of S_________ signed by parent or teacher

Answers: P=Pride, F=Folder 1. Goal(s) 2. Dedication 3. Student 4. Character 5. Awards 6. Papers 7. Support

How Do You Organize a Pride Folder?

Your first effort to make folders might be to have materials available and let the students do the following with the cover:

- Draw themselves and finger paint their handprints.
- Draw the school mascot with the word PRIDE across the top.
- Write their names into an acrostic with each letter a positive character trait.
- Glue a photograph into the middle of a crest with their values around it.

THEN

- Store them in a crate for easy access by them or you.
- Color-code the folders (if you need folders for more than one class).
- Provide a stapler, if you could not get folders with pockets to attach the initial goals sheet, copies of your Professional Educator Dedication Statement (PEDS), the Student's Dedication Statement (SDS), and parent support letter signed by them or the teacher.
- Have someone assigned to pass out the PRIDE FOLDERS each day (or Monday AM) so students can focus on their primary purpose and settle in.

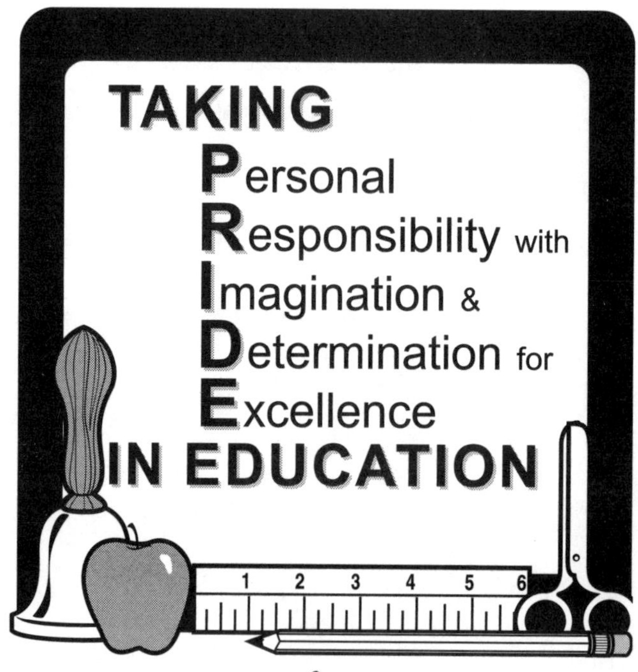

www.dianaday.com • 972-278-7773

What Do You Do When New Students Arrive Weekly?

Consistent Discipline

Having a constant stream of new students and maintaining a consistent discipline policy is like trying to herd cats. It seems impossible.

Here's the Answer

You could solve the problem of new students constantly needing to be inducted into your management plan by enlisting the skills and creativity of your stable population of students. Try this:

Video Tape Students Explaining Classroom Management Plan & PRIDE Folders

After your plan is in place the first week of school:

- ❑ Put students into small teams
- ❑ Explain that a video tape is going to be made for new students to view to understand both their Classroom Management Plan & PRIDE folders
- ❑ Have each group explain one section of the plan very carefully and seriously
    - Purpose of the PRIDE folder
    - Contents of the PRIDE folder
    - Why Plan created
    - Expectations (Rules)
    - How Behavior Management Plan Was Created & By Whom
    - Learning Choices (Limits)
    - Learning Incentives (Rewards)
    - Parent Support Letters (SDS & Discipline)
    - Closing Will Be Done By teacher
- ❑ Allow one less serious-minded, but creative group, to surprise the others by creating a "school commercial"
    - Select "Good Will Ambassadors" to show the school commercial video to new students and answer questions
    - Show the video at Open House to parents
    - Share this video with primary teachers whose students may be too young to create such a video

Date ______________________

Dear Parents of ______________________________,

My students and I believe that each of us is important and unique. Each of us has special talents and abilities. I am encouraging your child to pursue opportunities that far exceed my curriculum to reach his or her own personal goals and destiny.

You can help in this process. Please have each family member sign a copy of your child's <u>Goals Sheet</u>. Each of you will support the positive actions, determination and efforts of your child. Also remembering to send "You can do it" messages, will encourage your child to achieve everything he or she can dream.

Thanks for helping me to inspire your son or daughter to become all that he or she can be.

Sincerely,

Educator

I have read _____________'s Goals Sheet. I will give support through positive actions for his/her determination and efforts to reach the goals. I will always encourage and believe in my child's hopes and dreams.

_________________________ Family Member

_________________________ Family Member

_________________________ Family Member

_________________________ Family Member

_________________________ Family Member

_________________________ Family Member

Date ______________

Fecha ________________

Estimados Padres de ______________________________,

Mis estudiantes y yo pensamos que cada uno de nosotros es único e importante y tiene habilidades y talentos especiales. Estoy alentando a su hijo(a) a perseguir oportunidades que rebasen el plan de estudios para asi alcanzar sus metas personales y su destino.

Ustedes pueden ayudar en este proceso. Por favor, pidale a cada miembro de su familia que firme la Declaracion de Éxito del Estudiante de su hijo(a). Cada uno de ustedes podrá apoyar las acciones positivas, la determinación y los esfuerzos realizados por su hijo(a). También podrán ayudarlo(a) recordando el mandarle mensajes que digan "Yo puedo hacerlo", los cuáles animarán a su hijo(a) a llevar a cabo todo lo que haya soñado.

Gracias por ayudarme a inspirar a su hijo(a) a llegar a ser todo lo que pueda ser.

Atentamente,

Maestro(a)

Estamos enterados de la Declaración de Éxito de ______________________. Le apoyaremos con actitudes positivas para que, con su esfuerzo, pueda alcanzar las metas de la Declaración de Éxito. Siempre alentaremos y creerémos en los sueños y deseos de nuestro hijo(a).

______________________	______________________
Miembro de la familia	Miembro de la familia
______________________	______________________
Miembro de la familia	Miembro de la familia
______________________	______________________
Miembro de la familia	Miembro de la familia

Fecha __________

Problem-Solving Using the Goals Sheet Script

Is this your Pride Folder? Goal Sheet? {Adult smiling}

What are your goals?

If answer is:

Do you still want to reach that goal?

(Yes.) **Good!**

(No.) **Would you like to raise your goal** (pause), **lower it** (pause), **or** (nodding) **keep it the same?**

A 15%er's Response → *(I don't know.)* **There are three words that we never say when we talk about our goals. Do you know what those words are?**

(I don't know.) **That's right, they are, 'I don't know.' Would you like to raise your goals** (pause), **lower them** (pause) **or** (nodding) **keep them the same?**

A 5%er's Response → *(I don't care.)* **Let me get this straight. Did you say that you 'don't care'? I can't stand by and allow you not to care and possibly keep others from learning. I can't make you care, but if you choose not to work, then you will not be able to stay with the learners. Please take your supplies and move to ____________. Thank you.**

Do you remember my Dedication Poster? (Yes.)
Did I say that I wanted to help you reach your goals? (Yes.)

Look at my eyes. Do I look angry?
I'm not angry so I need you to keep looking at me as we speak.
All I want is your cooperation. Thank you.

When you (state the misbehavior), does it help you or hurt you to reach your goal? (Hurts me.)

Elementary: **Are you going to (state the correct behavior) or are you going to (state the misbehavior)?**

Secondary: **What are you going to do about (state the misbehavior)?**

Both: **You've made a good decision. Do you need any help with your work? I'll be back in a couple of minutes to see how you're doing. Remember, I'm here to help you. Thanks.**

Quarter-Minute Conferences to Get Kids Refocused

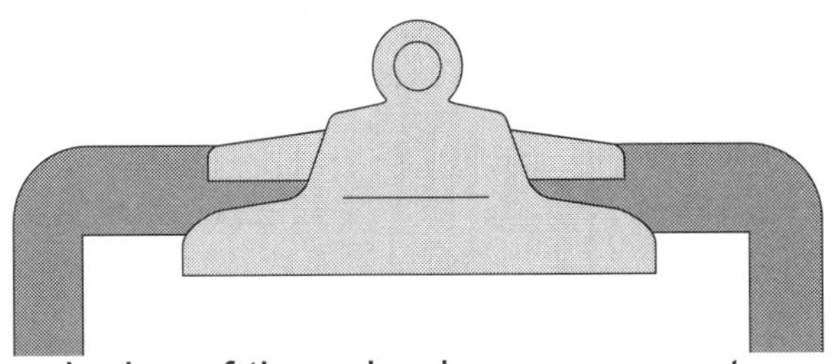

- "At the beginning of the school year, you wrote a goal and I committed to helping you reach it. What is your goal? What can you do to get back on track?"

- "My goal is to make a difference in your life and I won't let anything or anyone keep me from helping you."

- "When you tease Mary, are you moving toward your goals or away from them? Are you hurting her and keeping her from her goals? What is something that would help Mary to feel better? What do you need to do to get back on goal?"

- "You said you came to school to learn and have fun. When you're in the Principal's office, you aren't doing either. Let's get back to learning <u>and</u> having fun."

- "I can't allow our class to be disrupted. I have a dedication statement in everyone's PRIDE folder that says I will do whatever it takes for all of us to be successful."

- "Do you want any help to reach your goals with this lesson?

- "Rob, let's look at your PRIDE folder. Do you remember your goal? Do you still want to reach that goal? What do you think you need to do to reach it?"

- "Do you remember my dedication statement? I said I would do whatever it would take to help you. That can be helping you in class, helping you after class or at recess. You decide. When do you want the help? Can I help you now?"

Siftin' Time Is Here!

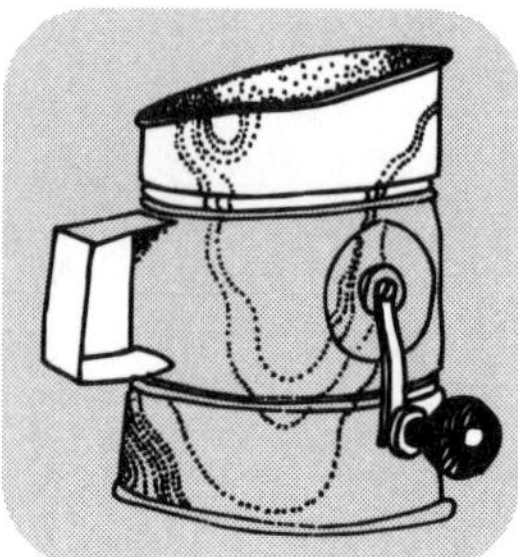

What exciting way will you teach goal setting to your students?

How will they keep their goals?
Pride folder, Agenda, Individual Goal Sheets in a Master Binder for specials?

When will you initiate problem-solving with a Goals Sheet? (page 54)

www.dianaday.com • 972-278-7773

Chapter 5

The Plan Hangs in the Balance

Creating Realistic Expectations

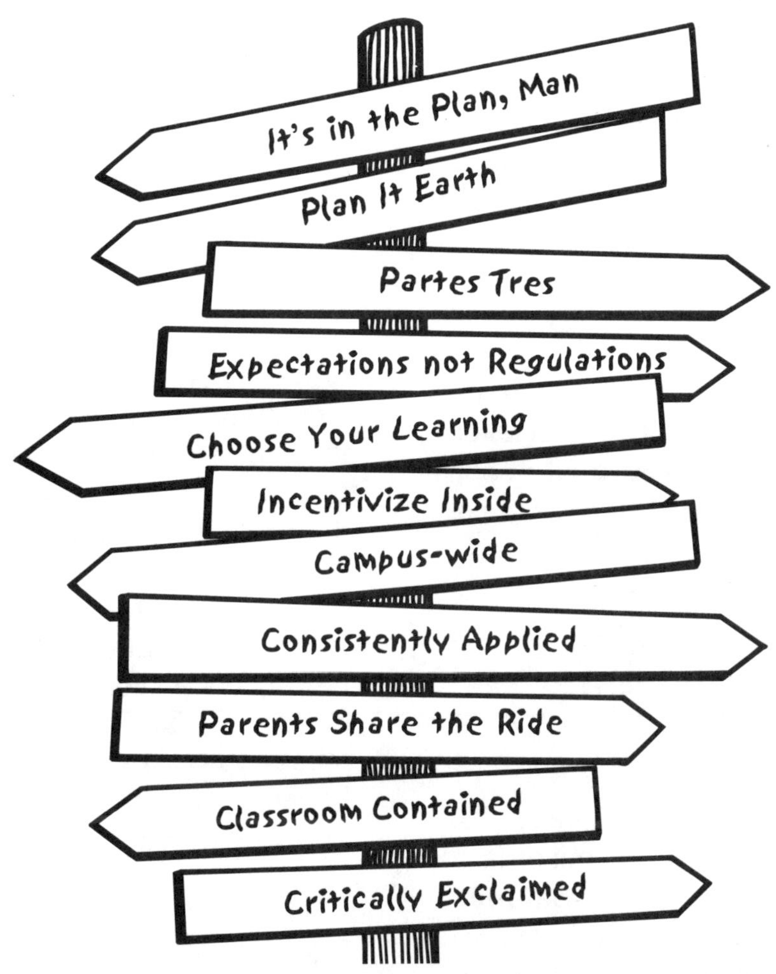

"The teacher who ignores expectations, becomes the lowest common denominator and lowers the standards of the school."

KEY ELEMENTS OF A CLASSROOM MANAGEMENT PLAN

3 Parts to a Plan

There are three parts to a behavior management plan. It is composed of **expectations** (formerly called rules) which are the "base" of your plan. Your "expectations" support the other two parts of your plan ("learning choices" and "learning incentives"). It is the most important part of your plan. Without well-written and well thought-out expectations, a discipline plan has no substance. Therefore, expectations must be broad enough to encompass a wide array of situations, but also very clear and concise.

If you create expectations that are too low, your students will bottom out at that level. **Raise the bar as high as you can!** Teach your students they must rise to the highest levels of their capability.

> *"If we do not expect excellence from them, who will?"*

Look at the illustration on page 73. Across the top of the fulcrum, or base, is a balance beam. If you have a **balance between learning choices** (formerly known as negative consequences or punishment) **and learning incentives** (formerly known as positive consequences or rewards), the bar comfortably rests on the base without a problem. It can spin on its base in any horizontal direction and still remain balanced. In other words, staff members can have different learning choices and incentives appropriate to their grade levels and degree of personal patience, and the school's consistency remains intact.

The "Base" Is the Key

The base is the most important part of the plan. All staff **must** have the same expectations. Everywhere students go on your campus, they must anticipate the same high expectations. Posted expectations from classroom to classroom must be worded exactly the same…no variation.

> *"Students must learn that all staff work together."*

Students must learn that all staff work together. All staff know what is expected of students and expect that high level of behavior. It allows for all staff to correct any student who does not perform to the expected standard of behavior.

Vision Management© stresses that learning incentives should not be based heavily upon stickers, stars, stamps, treats or free-time. Who has any "free time"? A few of those costly rewards will have a greater benefit if students do not expect to get them for every appropriate thing they do.

A learning incentive can be any of the following: to learn in a non-standard area of the room/campus, have a review of material that is competitive between two sides of the room and has the rules of a baseball or football game, hear a mind teaser or thought-provoking article the last minute of class, receiving a paper trophy for reaching one's goal, reviewing one's goals and making a "to-do" list. Everything on this list enhances the relationship between the teacher and students. **Students rarely act out in classrooms where firm limits and warm relationships exist.**

THE 3 PARTS OF A CLASSROOM MANAGEMENT PLAN

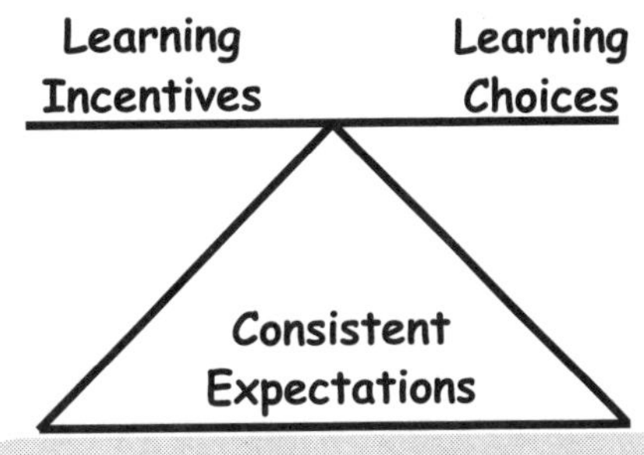

School functions with few problems
High respect for authority
High celebration of achievement

What do you think happens on a campus when the beam tilts?

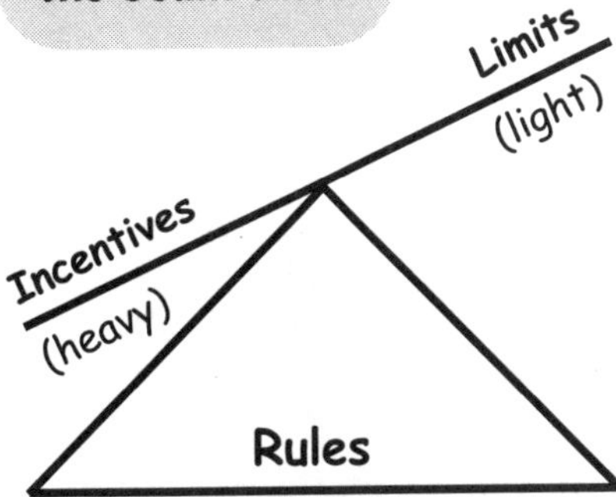

Poor follow-through by staff/administrators
Little respect for authority
Unearned celebration

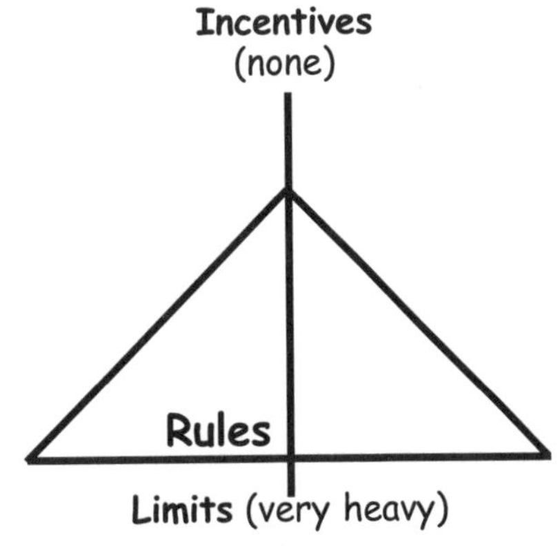

Very punitive environment
No reinforcement for progress
Vandalism likely

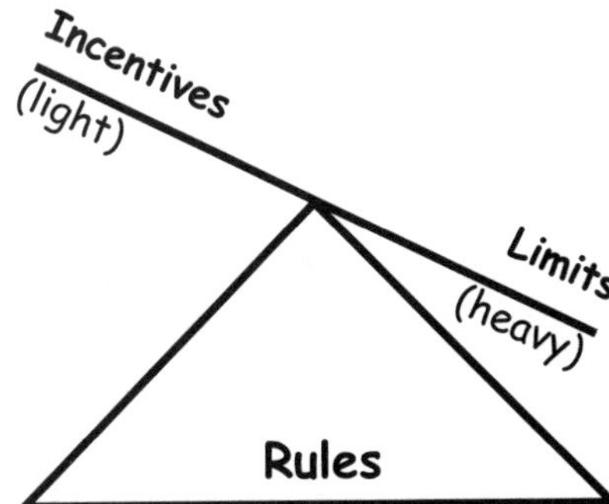

Covert misbehavior
Unhappy staff & students
Distrust
Little appreciation or celebration

A behavior management plan alone cannot make your students behave. It must be balanced with celebration, problem-solving & learning choices.

TEACHING, LIKE LIFE, IS A BALANCING ACT, TOO

"Anybody can make just about anything of himself if he really wants, and makes up his mind, to do it. We are capable of greater things than we realize. How much one actually achieves depends largely upon:

1. Desire 2. Faith 3. Persistent Effort 4. Ability

But if you're lacking the first three factors, your ability will not balance the lack. So concentrate on the first three and the results will amaze you."

Norman Vincent Peale

Guidelines for Schoolwide Expectations

Essential for Unity

It is essential that your staff display unity by posting and teaching the same expectations (rules) in every classroom or location in the school. If someone feels strongly that he requires an additional expectation, and it is not on the list, that is alright. As long as it meets the criteria below, and that individual has only one or two additional expectations, there will be no problem with schoolwide consistency.

"Everyone posting and teaching the same expectations is essential for unity."

Follow These Guidelines When Deciding Your Expectations:

- Post 5-6 classroom expectations
- Have only observable expectations
- Test your expectations with the "see" or "hear" rule which means you must either be able to see or hear the expectation to be followed or broken
- Discuss with students what each expectation means
- Role-play what it means to follow or not follow each expectation for complete understanding
- Check for understanding

A Role-Play Example

Role-Play

(Teacher says to students)

"Mark and Amy, come to the front of the room and stand by the door. If the expectation is for you to be in your assigned seats, with supplies, when the bell rings, show us what you would do. Now, show us what you would not do."

Check for Understanding

(Teacher says to students)

"If you purposely trip someone, which expectation have you broken?"

"If you are on time for class, which expectation have you followed?

Field-Tested Expectations

For Pre-School or Kindergarten

1. HFBO -- Keep hands, feet, books & objects to self.

2. Wait and think -- When someone is speaking, do not speak.

3. Stay with your class -- Do not leave without permission.

4. FMD -- Follow my directions.

FIELD-TESTED EXPECTATIONS (GRADES 1-12)

THE CHALLENGE TO EXCEL

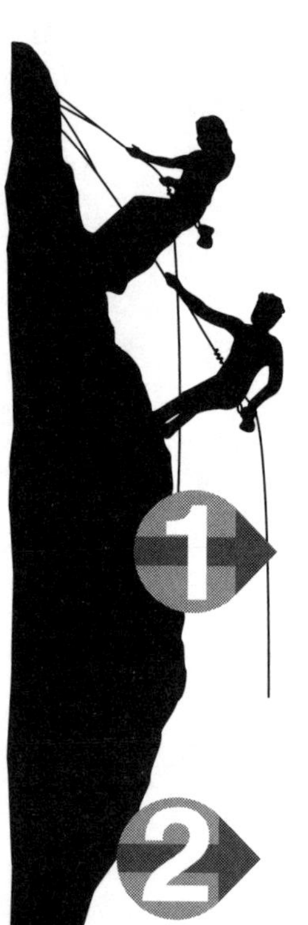

Classroom Expectations

1. Be in your assigned seat/area, ready to work when the bell finishes ringing.

2. Bring/Have paper, pencil, books and all needed materials every day.

3. HFBO--Keep hands, feet, books & objects to yourself.

4. No cussing, rude gestures, cruel teasing or put downs.

5. Follow directions of any adult working at this school.

What Is Critical Misbehavior?

Are there times when students refuse to cooperate?

Do some students refuse to stop disrupting?

Have you ever had students who refuse to leave their seat to go to a less stimulating area of the room so you can continue to teach?

Do you ever fear you or your students may not be safe?

It is vital that the faculty and administration are in agreement about what student behavior generates an office referral. A big reason for low teacher morale is when this is not made clear to staff and they are forced to "tough it out" with severely misbehaving students.

When students who stop the learning process are allowed to remain in the classroom, it sends a clear message to other students that misbehavior will be tolerated. It communicates, "The standards are low in this school. The teacher is powerless. Do whatever you want here." Students, who would never have been disruptive, will model other students' negative behavior.

Nonetheless, do not use the office as a dumping ground, either. The administrator does not have magical powers to "fix" difficult students. In fairness to both teachers and administrators, sending the student to any place where there is supervision will give the teacher some needed relief. It also sends the message, "Disruptive behavior will not be tolerated. We expect your cooperation for me to provide you an education."

> *"The administrator does not have magic dust..."*

It is important to be unified about what misbehavior generates an immediate office referral. **The following is considered critical misbehavior:**

1. Fighting or threatening to fight
2. Damaging or destroying student, teacher or school property
3. Overtly refusing to do school work when capable by throwing materials, tipping over furniture or yelling
4. Engaging in behavior that creates an unsafe situation, is sexually provocative or shuts down your ability to continue to teach

Classroom Expectations vs. Critical Expectations

Classroom Expectations

A "classroom expectation" refers to the five (5) expectations you use to manage your classroom.

(Suggested list on pages 75-76)

Critical Expectations

A "critical expectation" refers to the four (4) expectations that generate a referral to the office.

(Suggested list on page 77)

The Tent of Expectations

Look at the illustration on page 79. A tent is held together by a seam down the middle. The left side represents your five classroom expectations. It is your duty to hone the management skills that are required to hold up your half of the tent. Please put a "5" in the left circle.

"For now, believe you can do it!"

There is a strong stake holding the tent in place to keep it secure. The stake represents your learning choices, i.e., what you will do when students refuse to go back on-task upon your request. In the next chapter you will learn to do this. **For now, believe you CAN DO it.**

The right side of the tent represents the four critical expectations. Please put a "4" in the right circle. This is your administrator's half of the tent. It is the duty of the administrator to support staff when students get out-of-control and need supervision that is outside of the regular classroom. This is required to hold up this half of the tent. If either side of the tent lets down, the entire tent will fall down.

When sent to the office, the person who sees students is to ask for the Pride Folder or Goals Sheet. Be sure to send it. The adult in-charge can review with students their goals, action steps, the referral slip sent by the teacher, problem-solve new behavior, and provide a learning choice to these students for being so disruptive to have been sent from the classroom. All of this is required to hold up the right side of the tent.

"The adult in-charge can review with the student his goals, action steps."

Classroom Expectations vs. Critical Expectations

Return to Sender

Appreciate the person who does "behind-the-scenes" effort. A child's behavior does not miraculously change. Someone in your building will need to put forth great effort to turn this child around.

If the child begins to disrupt upon return to the classroom, **SEND HIM BACK TO THE SAME PERSON.** It is likely that this student has made promises to this adult about changing the behavior that got him to the office. The student must return and acknowledge that he did not keep his word. The adult will go through the entire process, applying more serious learning choices. **This step rarely happens because...**

Few teachers send students back to the office, perhaps thinking, "Nothing got fixed last time." Please, send them back! If you do not, the students have learned, "If I keep it up, I wear them down and then nothing happens."

Cries for Help

Remember: If the student is 7, 10, or 17 years old, it took him that many years to acquire those misbehaviors and a self-defeating attitude. The problems are not going to be "fixed" with one, two or even three referrals or counseling sessions. Do not give up on these students. They are the ones who are crying out for help the most by their outrageous behavior.

Do you see the stake that holds the right side of the tent safe and secure? This stake represents the problem-solving and learning choices that will occur at the office level.

It is important that the office has a **systematic list** of what will happen each time a student is sent on a critical referral. Then, there can be no misunderstanding by either student or parent as to what is going to happen if the misbehavior continues. Claims of prejudice, lack of fairness fly-out the window.

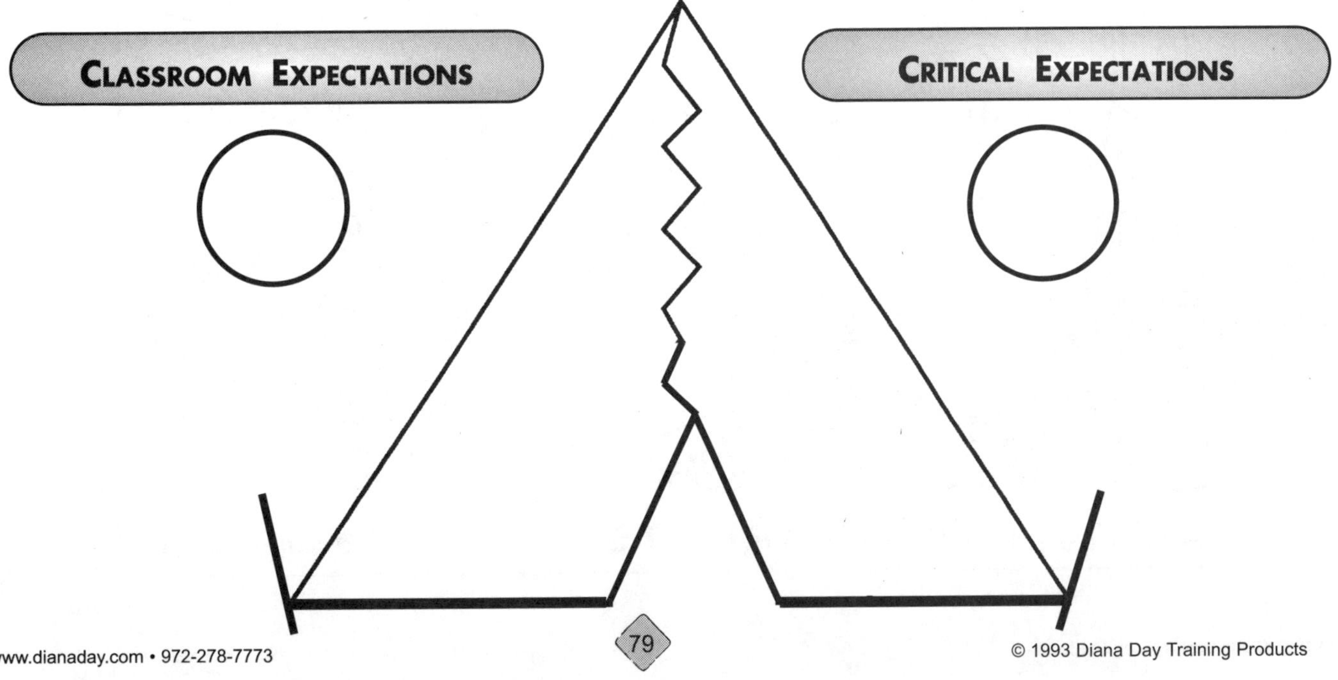

When Is No News Not Good News?

Most Parents Will Support the Teacher if They:

- Believe you like their child.
- Trust that you are working in their child's best interest.
- Have had positive communication from you periodically--not just continuous negative contact.

As you know, students are not keen about taking notes home that:

1). Outline the teacher's behavior management plan for the parents

2). Report misbehavior

Which of your students is least likely to take behavior notes or the management plan letter home to be signed? Yes, the one who most needs the communication delivered.

Before the Letter Goes Home:

- Go over the communication thoroughly with the student.
- Emphasize that the student tell parent(s) that they know what the note says and will take responsibility for what happened.
- Remind student that it's a joint effort to have a safe & orderly place to learn.
- Tell student you will call at a specific time and the student is to answer the phone, telling you the parents have been informed. Then, speak to the parents.

Dear Parent (Family Member),

It is a pleasure to have _______________ in my _______________ class this year. You recently signed _______________'s Goal Sheet. I know you are as pleased as I am about his/her plan. With enthusiasm and energy, I will guide your child to meet those goals and also to make responsible decisions.

To reach our goals, the class and I need a safe and orderly place to learn. Each student is asking a family member to sign this *Vision Management©* Plan.

Student Expectations

1. Be in your assigned seat/area, ready to work when the bell finishes ringing.
2. Bring/Have paper, pencil, books and all needed materials every day.
3. HFBO--Keep hands, feet, books & objects to yourself.
4. No cussing, rude gestures, cruel teasing or put downs.
5. Follow directions of any adult working at this school.

YOUR CHILD'S EDUCATION

Encouragement

You and I have the important responsibility to encourage and support your child. He/she can achieve what can be dreamed. Our mutual desire is to help your child enjoy the good times and learn from the tough times.

Learning Choices

Occasionally, students ignore classroom expectations. I will give students cues, reminders and will redirect them to focus on their work to get them back on track. When the misbehavior continues, the following will occur:

Reminder ____________________

Cue ____________________

Redirect(s) ____________________

____________________ ____________________

____________________ ____________________

For a serious disruption such as fighting, destroying property, refusing to work or for serious defiance, your child would be sent to the Principal. You would be contacted to come to school and your child counselled.

I look forward to meeting you and giving you much good news.

____________________ __________ ____________

Teacher's Signature Date Class

- -

I have read and discussed the behavior management plan with my child. I know I am welcome at school anytime I want to help out or to talk about a concern for my child.

Parent/Guardian Signature ____________________ **Date** __________

Student Signature ____________________ **Phone #** __________

Message back to teacher ____________________

____

Estimados Padres (Miembros de la Familia):

Es un placer tener a _______________________ este año en mi clase. Usted firmó recientemente la Declaración de Éxito de ___________________ y sé que deben estar tan gustosos como yo de sus objetivos. Con/entusiasmo con entusiasmo y energía guiaré a su hijo/a a lograr esos objetivos y también a tomar decisiones responsables.

Para alcanzar esos objetivos, nuestra clase ha desarrollado el siguiente plan. Cada estudiante aportó ideas para hacer de nuestro salón de clases un lugar estimulante y seguro para aprender.

Expectativas del Estudiante

1. Esté en el asiento asignado/área, se prepara para trabajar cuando los fines de la campana sonando.
2. Traiga/tiene papel, el lápiz, los libros y todas materias necesitadas todos los días.
3. Mantiene manos, los pies, los libros & objetos a usted mismo.
4. Ningún cussing, los gestos groseros, molestar cruel ni puso hacia abajo.
5. Siga las direcciones de cualquier trabajar adulto en esta escuela.

Ánimo

Ustedes y yo tenemos la importante responsabilidad de animar y apoyar a su hijo/a. Él/ella puede lograr lo que ha soñado. Nuestro deseo mutuo es de ayudar a su hijo/a a disfrutar los momentos buenos y a aprender de los malos.

Decisiones Para Aprender

Ocasionalmente los estudiantes ignoran las expectativas del salón de clases. Les daré señas, recordatorios y advertencias para regresarlos al camino correcto. Cuando el comportamiento continúa, ocurrirá lo siguiente:

Recordatorio ______________________________
Seña ______________________________
Advertencia ______________________________
______________________________ ______________________________
______________________________ ______________________________

Por uná interrupción seria como el pelearse, destruir la propiedad, rehusarse a trabajar o un desafío severo, su hijo/a irá a el/la principal, y se le avisará losa padres y su hijola sera aconsejado/a.

Estoy deseoso/ a de llamarlos y enviarles notas con muchas buenas noticias durante este año!

_________________ _________ ___________
Firma del Maestro/a Fecha Clase

He leído y discutido con mi hijo/ a las expectativas del salón de clases. Sé que soy bienvenida en la escuela a cualquier hora que quiera ayudar o hablar sobre alguna preocupación relacionada con mi hijo/a.

Firma del Padra/Encargado ________________________________ Fecha _____________
Firma del Estudiante ________________________________ # del telefono _____________
Mensaje para el/la Maestrola ____
____

Come On Let's Sift Again Like We Did Last Summer

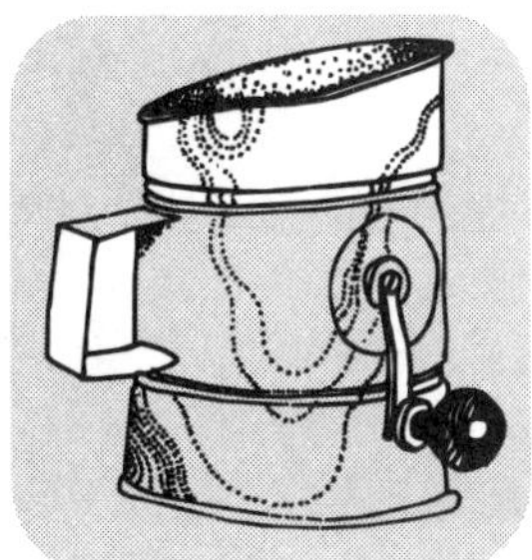

Write one of the expectations you think your most difficult students will not follow.

Write it here.

How will you teach this expectation?

What specific behavior will you model to students to show them the right way to act?

What role-play will you set up to practice this proper behavior?

"Ever a Role Model"

You're working very hard.
Me, I'm just cruisin'.
I think I'm a winner,
but you know that I'm losin'.

You try to show me
the way that I should go.
But I don't care to listen,
'cuz, man, I'm in the know.

Why should I trust you?
You're just workin' for pay.
Just like everyone else,
you'll give-up on me one day.

But, then, you start to reach me
and you don't even know,
Your kindness and patience
are the seeds to help me grow.

Please, just keep trying.
Do not be dissuaded.
In case you haven't noticed,
I'm not easily persuaded.

You think I've been ignoring you
every step along the way.
When actually I've been watching
your step each and every day.

So little-by-little
I start reaching for the stars.
No longer prone to worry
about those hurtful scars.

You must be very special
to care the way you do.
And, maybe, you are right,
I AM SPECIAL, TOO!

Rick Pehrson

Are you a role model or a troll model?

Chapter 6

The Power of Simple Solutions

Using Two Steps to Solve a Problem

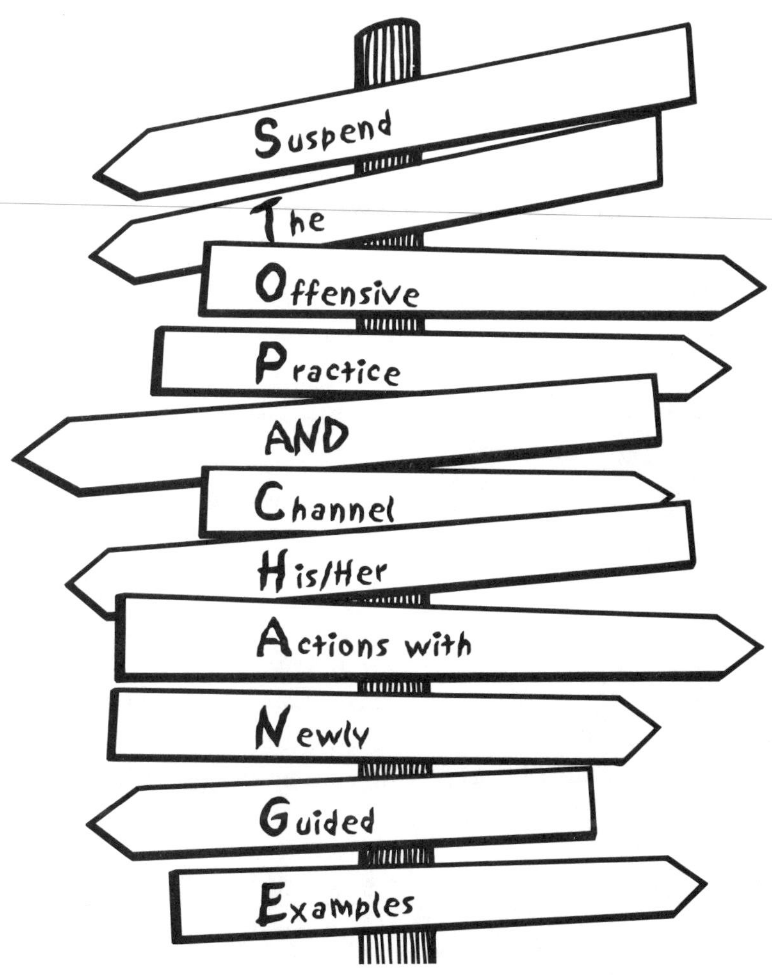

"Work joyfully and peacefully,
knowing that right thoughts and right efforts
will inevitably bring about right results."

James Allen

WHAT'S A DISCIPLINE HIERARCHY?

Due Process

A "discipline hierarchy" is a name commonly used for the list of learning choices in your behavior management plan. Legally, you are informing your students what will happen the first, second, third or 99th time they refuse to cooperate. When you make this list and explain it to your students,it is legally known as **"due process."**

Some discipline hierarchies begin with a "warning," then three strikes and you are OUUUT of the room. No questions may be asked. No answers will be given. That worked

> *"Scare tactics stopped working after the last rerun of 'Leave It to Beaver.'"*

fine when students were afraid of us. Today, a typical response might be, "Give me a thousand strikes! I don't care." Scare tactics stopped working after the last episode of "Leave It To Beaver."

Focus on Goals

Give your discipline hierarchy careful consideration. It is not meant to embarrass, humiliate, break the spirit, make eat crow,

> *"Your discipline hierarchy is meant to get your students to calm down."*

inflict shame, guilt or pain. It is meant to get your students to calm down. They are to think and process about what is expected and contrast that to what they are doing. They are to refocus...back to your expectations and their GOALS! If they no longer want the goal they previously wrote, have already achieved it, or need to change it, suggest they prepare a new goal sheet of what they do want.

Some students have a need to "push the envelope." They refuse to comply to see if you are going to follow your discipline hierarchy. Answer: DO IT. Do you see why you must put time and effort into your plan? It's because students will be testing you to use it...often!

When students disobey, they frequently say they "forgot" what was expected. Very young children might "forget," but older students rarely do.

What's a Learning Choice?

Punishment Is Out

Students chronically misbehave because they are used to many reprimands by teachers who do not back up their words with actions. As long as these teachers deliver meaningless threats, students will continue to ignore their directions.

> *"As long as teachers deliver meaningless threats, students will continue to ignore their directions."*

Learning Choices Are In

Using your *Vision Management©* plan correctly, you will request a student to refocus on his task. If he/she continues to misbehave, take an action called a **"learning choice."** A "learning choice" is a term we use instead of "punishment," "negative consequence," "logical consequence" or "setting-limits." **It means that the student is choosing to learn from another location.** Once students understand its full meaning, as defined in this chapter, they accept the learning choice because it is not punitive.

Move 'Em or Lose "em

Moving the disruptive student to another location, hopefully within your classroom, is an important learning choice. You cannot make the student learn,

> *"You cannot make the student learn..."*

but you can make sure that he does not stop others from learning. It needs to be made clear to the class that no one student, or group of students, will be allowed to stop the learning process of other students. No one has the right to impede the success of anyone's personal plan to achieve and learn, including your plan to teach.

Guidelines for Learning Choices

- You are comfortable with all your learning choices, and will consistently apply them.
- You have checked that the plan complies with school or district policy.
- You have built problem-solving and refocusing steps into the plan.
- You are including a level where parent involvement is required—a contact or conference.
- You have considered the age appropriateness of your plan.

No More Time for Time-Out

Build Cooperation

Use the word, "learning choice," instead of "negative consequence," because it is less harsh and will get you far more cooperation. An example of a negative consequence used in most classrooms, K-12, is a "time-out."

> ***Students think time-out is: "A place to go when you're bad or punished."***

When asked to define the word, "time-out," students of all levels said, "a place to go when you're bad or punished." In the past, some teachers informed students that they "did not exist" at that location, "would not receive help," nor "could they ask a question." What would entice a student to want to behave when treated in such a manner? In this decade, they are not buying the old, punitive methods.

The Goal: Refocus

Explain to your students that if they "choose to learn" from another place in the room or campus, it is not meant as punishment. In fact, it might be called "Australia," "Able Table," or "The Beach." It has an acceptable name because it is a good, alternative place to go when students are having a difficult time adjusting to classroom expectations. It is an invitation to students to move in order to better focus on what they wrote on their goal sheet.

When the student has refocused, or self-managed, which means stopped the refusal or disruptive behavior, he is likely to participate in the lesson, ask questions, do the work—**all from his new location in the room.** However, before returning to his former location, he needs to request a moment from the teacher to reaffirm his commitment to go back on goal. The teacher asks, "What happened that got you here? What will your new behavior be when you return to the learning area?"

> ***"Student needs to reaffirm commitment to go back on goal."***

That's it. The student goes back to his seat having put himself on-track. He is becoming self-managed! If the teacher uses the proper management style when addressing the student, the student will cooperate and learn to manage himself.

STUDENTS CAN HELP NAME THE "REFOCUSING LOCATION"

What's In a Name?

Banish from your vocabulary the word, "time-out." Today's students will not go to a place called "time-out." It's one of those words from the dinosaur age. Ask students which areas of the classroom could be used to think or refocus. If they choose the floor, corner hideaway, or a lab area, then they approve of it and are likely to go there when you request it.

Ask students to give "a name" to each of the refocusing locations they chose. They are amazingly humorous and clever at this.

The Name Game

Names that have been commonly chosen are:

Jupiter
Pluto
Thinking Zone
Johnny Mathis
Perry Como
Lawrence Welk
Humpty Dumpty
Little Jack Horner
Three Little Kittens
Mozart, Beethoven, Bach
North Pole, South Pole
B-Flat, C Sharp
Locations of Olympic Games - for P.E.
Back Street, Port of Entry, Customs
Fargo (students need to "go far")
Alaska (students who refuse, think they are cool, so they need to go someplace cold to refocus)
Thinking Tree
Think Chair
Able Table
Burger King
Mr. Goodburgers
Taco Bell
Cloud 9
Heaven

The Humor Mill

Humor can take the rough corners off an edgy situation. Sometimes, both student and teacher chuckle as the teacher asks the

student to move to a place with a silly name, especially when it's not meant to punish but to refocus.

> *"Richard, please move to the Pearly Gates."*

Learning Choices for Your Discipline Hierarchy

Had a Bad Hair Day?

It's time to decide what you require for learning choices when students refuse to cooperate. Do not rush to judge the motivation of a "refuser," nor to convict him.

- Have you ever had a personal bad day or bad minute?
- Have you ever said something with a harsh tone that you later wished you hadn't?
- Have you refused a request and later regretted it?

If you have, join the one hundred-fifty million students who occasionally do, too. The problem is, for some students, a personal bad day may be a daily occurrence. There is no need for you to over-react or take it personally. When you manage your students effectively and consistently, the acting-out behaviors will occur less frequently.

"These learning choices should work smoothly for you."

Learning Choice #1 The "Pre-Minder"

No, it's not a typo. A **"pre-minder"** is a **"prompt"** that you give to students well before they make another poor decision. Who receives a "pre-minder?" Have you ever had a student whom you could predict would misbehave in your room? Not only could you predict who would misbehave, but also knew what the misbehavior would be? Choose to give pre-minders to students who make the same poor decision or display the same misbehavior daily.

As the student is entering the classroom, politely take him aside for the following, private conversation:
(The student chronically does not have supplies and walks around.)

The first day, say:

"Name, Good morning! We are going to begin our day with a brain teaser that refers to yesterday's material.
I want you to get a pencil out of the stub can, if you need one, and get paper. Then, go directly to your seat.
(Smile) What do I want you to do?
Yes.Thanks!"

The next day, say:

"Name, Good morning! We are going to have a pop quiz with open notes.
I want you to get a pencil from where?
What else will you need? Yes!
Then, where do you directly go? Yes!
(Smile) Thanks!"

Learning Choices for Your Discipline Hierarchy

Learning Choice #1
The "Pre-Minder"

The next day, say:

"Name, Good morning!
We are going to begin with an exercise we copy from the board.
I want you to do what? Yes!
You also need what? Yes!
Then, you go where? Yes!
(Smile) Thank you!"

The next day, say:

"Name, Good morning!
We are going to write in our journals right away. You are. (point to the student while smiling) Yes!
You are also. Yes!
Then, you'll. Yes!
Thanks!"

The next day, say:

"Name, Good Morning!
We are going to learn how to take notes when doing an interview with a partner.
You. (wait for answer) Yes!
You. (wait for answer)Yes!
You. (wait for answer) Yes!
Thanks!"

The next day, say:

"Name, Good morning!
We are having our chapter test today.
Yes! Yes! Yes!
Thanks, name, I hope you do well on your test. I'm rooting for you!"

Keep this up for as many as 21 days! It has been said that it takes 21 days to create a habit. You want the student to see your face and think, "I need pencil and paper and need to go directly to my seat." He'll be 89 years old and you'll be 119, and he'll still remember your face and think about needing paper, pencil and moving directly to his seat (in the nursing home).

Pre-minders are very effective.

WHY "RE-MINDERS" DO NOT WORK

- They are given after a student has forgotten, or never intended to do it.
- Students are used to ignoring their parents.
- Reminders given loudly across the room are viewed as a threat.
- Students who get many different reminders feel nagged at and rebel.
- It may teach a student not to have to think because he'll be reminded anyway.

Learning Choices for Your Discipline Hierarchy

Learning Choice #2
Cueing

Verbal Cueing

When a student is looking around…not engaged in you or your lesson, say the student's name as a part of the lesson. Do not do this to embarrass or thinking, "Gotcha," but to focus the student back to the lesson. If many students are looking around not engaged, sorry, it is your stink-o lesson. It, and you, may need some energy to breathe life back into the students.

Examples of verbal cueing are:
"Christopher Columbus, who may be related to our Christopher Keith Lawrence, asked Queen Isabella to fund his voyage to go around the world."

(Troy is talking across the aisle.)
"Troy knows the answer and wants to know if Stacy does, too. Stacy, what is the name of the country that used to be called Burma?"

"When Jasmine looks at this math problem, she knows she has to ..."

> *"Smiling, while cueing, shows that you are not angry..."*

Smiling, while cueing, shows that you are not angry, but do want the student to refocus.

Body Cueing

- Stand near students who are incessant talkers.
- Pre-arrange a signal or a touch that has been agreed to between the student and yourself. When he begins to wander or talk-out, use it.
- Leave your Teacher's Guide on the corner of your most challenging student's desk. He knows you will be returning to give him attention. If you feel the insatiable urge to use a podium, use this student's desk instead!

Professor Magoo and his magical cue!

Learning Choices for Your Discipline Hierarchy

Learning Choice #2 Cueing

Visual Cueing

Using something like "the mean, hard stare" or the "neutral look" is really out of date unless you want to play the role of the schoolmaster in "The Little House on the Prairie."

You can send the best "stop it" message with your eyes, just by raising your eyebrows and widening your eyes...**never** narrowing them! It's called **"Big Eyes."** Hold the look for just a moment, and then look away, continuing to speak or walk around. Big eyes can also be done when you bend down to privately speak to a student. The student must always understand what your "look" means and what he is to do.

> ***"You can send the best 'stop it' message with your eyes."***

Answer Cueing

Have you ever been called on at a meeting of your peers and you just weren't "home"? How humiliating to admit to the group that you weren't listening. You explain that you were listening the second before...but...but...a fly, no, a roach...it could have been an ant was...

Don't we catch students tuning-out all the time? Save them by using "answer cueing." After waiting for an answer a comfortable amount of time, say, "I know you know this answer. The capital of Texas is an Awwwww...awesome place. There was a movie that was a man's name and the capital of Texas was his first name. Powers....Awwww-something Powers! Yes, you got it! Austin. I knew you knew it!"

> ***"Do you think students act better in classrooms where they have bonded with the teacher?"***

Do you think that student will be smiling? Do you think you've built a bond with that student? Do you think students act better in classrooms where they have bonded with the teacher? Answer cueing is fun for both the student and you. The entire class will enjoy this.

Learning Choices for Your Discipline Hierarchy

Learning Choice #3 Redirecting

Talk to Turn Around

A **"redirect"** is anything you do to direct a student back on-task. Cueing can actually be considered a form of redirection. The term, "redirect," means you talk with the student to encourage him to change his behavior. **Redirect when cueing does not work.**

"Redirect when cueing does not work"

Redirects are highly effective, and may be used over and over, as long as you have the patience. Never put a quantity on the number of redirects to use with any single student. It is up to you.

If you have many students who require redirecting, then the number you give an individual might be less because all you'd be doing is redirecting and never teaching.

Redirect Example

Let's say that a student was "pre-minded" about taking out supplies and doing work that he was capable of doing. When the class was settling into the work, this student still had not taken out supplies. The teacher cued him by praising a student nearby for working. The student continues to be non-productive.

The teacher is now going to use the third level of her discipline hierarchy...the learning choice called "redirect":

Redirect Script

1. **Move to student while others are working.**
2. **Bend over with "big eyes."**
3. **With a calm voice say, "Are you alright?** (wait) **Do you need any help?** (wait) **Then, let's go to work."**
4. **End with a small smile and a "thank you" while you walk away.**

"Most students will go back to work..."

The teacher is redirecting the student away from former behavior and into what is expected. Most students will go back to work when you use this approach.

Learning Choices for Your Discipline Hierarchy

Learning Choice #4
Move to Refocus Area

Mutiny in Your County?

If, after giving ample time, the student continues to refuse or disrupts, definitely move to the next level of your discipline hierarchy which would be to move his location in the room. The "learning choice" is to sit in an area of the room where he cannot affect others but can refocus. Even if he silently refuses, and you feel he isn't bothering anyone, the refusal of your request to move is contagious. Others will join the mutiny and refuse directions. Never allow students to refuse your directions.

"What if the student will not move?"

You may ask, **"What if he will not move?"** Give ample time, then move into the next level of your discipline hierarchy. Repeat the Redirect Script (page 94). The student will be highly resistant to change his seat if it's issued like a command, and with such volume, that other students can hear.

Be Captain Kindness

If the student is still refusing, say **"I can't force you to learn, or to move. But I'd be a poor teacher if I allow you to give others the message that it's alright not to learn in this school. You've decided to receive an office referral. Let's have a new start tomorrow. Thank you."**

"You've decided to have an office referral!"

You have shown strength of character by your action. You had a consistent response according to your discipline plan while you maintained the relationship between the student and you. The class sees that you will support students who stand by their goals and action plans to get ahead, and will not allow disrespect or refusal from others.

Remember that you cannot problem-solve with someone who will not communicate with you. Sometimes a disciplinary action is necessary to earn the respect of some students. Always do this calmly, without anger or sarcasm in your voice.

3 Core Beliefs of an Effective System

Have you ever been given these suggestions to manage your discipline problems?

- Smile more
- Be more calm
- Be at the door when students enter
- Reward them
- Move around
- Refigure retirement
- Change your seating arrangement
- Move to Tahiti
- Engage students in conversation so they'll talk to you and not one another

The above are strategies, not a management system. Used in isolation, none will work on their own except retirement to Tahiti. These are feeble attempts to help new and "needs improvement" teachers. Some ideas have merit but are simplistic attempts to solve some big management problems. But, without substantive training or resources, teachers may be forced to control their classes through anger and frustration. Unfortunately, emotions guide our actions.

> *"Simplistic strategies are no substitute..."*

In our personal life, we would not want to feel out-of-control and base our actions solely upon our emotions. So, we cannot allow ourselves to be out-of-control in the classroom either. Simplistic strategies are no substitute for a sound, effective behavior management system that is used consistently.

To help you use your management system consistently, there are three basic beliefs you must have:

Vision Management© Belief #1

When a situation is getting out-of-hand, and a student must be dealt with calmly and firmly, remember:

You can't s________ a problem d__________ a problem.

There are _______ steps necessary to solve a problem.

1. S____________ the misbehavior

2. C____________ the behavior

Are you firm and calm or jumpy and grumpy?

Answers: solve, during, two, Stop, Change

3 Core Beliefs of an Effective System

Vision Management© Belief #2

If you want to s_____ a misbehavior, consistently use a learning choice of pre-minding, cueing, redirecting or a location change. One of those is going to stop the disruption or refusal.

The problem is that **we never get around to changing the behavior** that went haywire in the first place. Perhaps, the student

> *"We never get around to changing the behavior..."*

got to return to his seat because a timer was set while he was in time-out. So, a chunk-of-plastic timer determined that this student was refocused enough to return to his former location. Why are we so surprised when the student starts his antics all over again when he returns to his seat? Gee, that hunk-of-junk-of-plastic worked 40 years ago so we thought it would work forever. The last time that worked, Roy Rogers used it on Trigger.

Vision Management© Belief #3

If you want to c_________ a behavior, support the student by having problem-solving sessions. These would

> *"Through modeling and role-plays, the student can be taught self-control."*

include going over his Goals Sheet, writing "How I'm Doing" form, or writing a new Goals Sheet specifically aimed at the problem that needs to get fixed. Several problem-solving sheets are in this book. Through modeling and role-plays, the student can be taught self-control. Certainly, notice and complement appropriate behavior when you see change.

To teach a new behavior, change from a controlling management style (Authoritarian, Parental, Monitor) that leads to punishment, to support, guidance and modeling of a Visionary Style. This will change the morale in the class and give you a much better school year.

Answers: stop, change

Refocus Sheet

Ask yourself these questions. Be ready to discuss them with your teacher prior to returning to class. Please answer them thoughtfully.

1. Why are you here?

2. What is your goal?

3. Is what you did helping or hurting you to reach your goal?

4. If you were to start the day all over again, what would you do differently? Tell in detail.

5. What is your plan when you go back to your area?

6. What do you think should happen if you refuse to follow directions again?

7. What is your parent's name and how can we contact your parent?

Your signature ___________________ Teacher's signature ___________________

Date _________________________

Copy to parent, if student continues

Parent signature ___________________

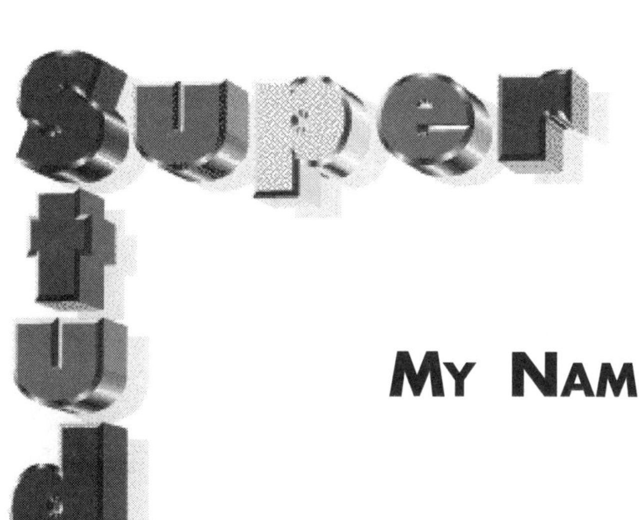

My Name:

____

My First Goal Is:

I need to:

Learning Choices - The BIG Picture

Review Your Options

Look at the three general categories of learning choices on page 101 to familiarize yourself with options that may be available to you when a student(s) refuses to cooperate in your class.

"Check to see if there are standardized procedures for managing chronically misbehaving students."

Then, talk with your grade level or department chairperson to see if there are standardized procedures for managing chronically misbehaving students that you will be expected to use. If you are told that staff members are allowed to devise their own learning choices (steps), do this:

9 Steps to Success with Learning Choices

1. Study the options under each category (pg. 101) and make a list of those you would be comfortable using.
2. Consider how many steps you want in your hierarchy because you must have the time, patience and energy to follow-through with each and every one.
3. Look at samples of hierarchies (pgs. 103-107).
4. Create one that is age and grade appropriate.
5. Set it aside for a day or two.
6. Reread your plan and see how it fits you.
7. Revise, if needed.
8. Print it on your Management Plan Poster.
9. Choose an interesting, non-threatening method to explain each level to your students.

Alternative Method!
(Not recommended)

Learning Choices - The BIG Picture

The 3 Categories of Learning Choices

These would be used if the student refused to cooperate through redirection, problem-solving and/or the student created an unsafe situation.

Loss or Delay of Privileges

* Denied participation in activities
* Denied use of educational equipment
* Denied access to areas in the school

Loss of Freedom or Required Interaction

* Denied interaction with other students
* Required attendance in another classroom
* Required reflection with writing time
* Required interaction with victim of his behavior
* Required interaction with family member
* Required interaction with school administration
* Required interaction with police

Restitution

* Repair of item(s)
* Replacement of item(s)
* Makes restitution to victim of behavior

Jerrold Gilbert- "Logical Consequences: A New Classification," *Journal of Individual Psychology*, 42 (no.2):243

Learning Choices - The DETAILED Picture

Creating Your Hierarchy

Following are examples of learning choice combinations that create a discipline hierarchy. Your hierarchy may have as many levels as you want. You may "clear" it (having the students start from the top of the hierarchy), whenever you wish. Make it age and grade appropriate.

> *"Your hierarchy may have as many levels as you want..."*

A suggestion is that primary grades (K-3) start over daily. Think this way: They are learning new procedures, independence, and, most importantly, self-control. Pre-K and K are likely to make mistakes as they learn "to sit still and be quiet."

Intermediate grades (4-6) have been practicing procedures, how to get along and self-discipline for a while now. Clear the slate once a week. However, have more levels in your discipline hierarchy before they are office-bound. They are likely to assert some independence to find out if you say what you mean and mean what you say.

Secondary Considerations

By the time students reach secondary (7-12), they are either settled into a routine of self-discipline, or not. Some will require little refocusing; some a lot. Adolescence initiates some odd types of acting out that you should not take personally. If you have chosen middle school, then enjoy their great senses of humor and "expect the unexpected" frequently. It is a fun level to teach.

Middle or junior high students can go about 3 weeks and high school students 6-9 weeks before starting over. Be sure to have a long enough hierarchy so you are not sending everyone to the office by the end of the first week. The purpose is to teach them to refocus quickly and to problem-solve independently or without your guidance. It is **not** about having office referrals in your holster, saying from across the room, "Make my day."

The following pages contain examples of hierarchies to guide you.

> "At any grade level, you may start fresh every day, as it may be simpler for you."

Learning Choices
Low Primary PK-1

Start over daily | **Create Your Hierarchy**

- **Preminder/Cue** – When possible
- **Redirect** – Private, verbal directions (Give as many redirects as you have patience to give)
- **Yellow Rug** – "Take the yellow rug and sit next to your goal sheet with your picture on it (hung on wall at height of child). Refocus and think about what you need to do differently." Have a 30-second teacher conference for student to say what he's going to do now. Set a timer for 3-5 minutes so you don't forget about him. If you are in the middle of a lesson do not feel you must attend to this child because the timer went off. Nod to the student. Go over when you can. Then ask, "Did you throw the toy? When you return, will you throw toys or play with them properly?"
  A correct response: Student returns to area.
  An incorrect response: Teacher **calmly** says, "I see you need more time to think about it."
- **Orange Rug** – Repeat of above with five minutes for refocus before checking on student
- **Red Rug** – Repeat of above with 10 minutes for refocus
- **Send to Buddy** – Send to another kindergarten class for 20 minutes and do a 30-second teacher conference, send a parent note home to be signed
- **Office** – Send with Goal Sheet, copy of referral goes home to be signed

My "Magic Dust" Seems to Be Out of Order

Learning Choices
Grades 2-6

Start over daily Gr. 2-3
Start over weekly Gr. 4-6

Create Your Hierarchy

- **Preminder/Cue** – When possible
- **Redirect** – Private, verbal directions
  (Give as many as you have patience to give)
- **Jupiter** – Take Pride Folder and assignment, have a 30-second refocus-to-goals with student.

  "What is your goal? When you __________ (misbehavior), does it help you to reach your goal? What are you going to do differently?"
- **Pluto** – Same as above and fill in Refocus Form
- **Send to buddy** – Same as above, but,
  write a different Refocus Form,
  stay a minimum of 30 minutes with buddy,
  make parent contact
- **Office Referral** – Send with Pride Folder, Refocus Forms, copy of referral goes home

____

____

____

____

____

____

____

____

____

____

____

____

____

____

____

____

____

____

____

Learning Choices Grades 7-12

Junior High Clears in 3 Weeks High School 6-9 Weeks

Create Your Hierarchy

(Each class period, redirect about 3 times. Then, apply the learning choice level that the student has reached.)

* **Pre-minder/Cue** – When possible
* **Redirect** – Private, verbal directions (Give as many as you have patience to give.)
* **Move away** from classmates. Move away for remainder of class period so others can learn.
  • Ask student to pull goal sheet from this class period's folder.
  • Thirty-second focus-to-goals with teacher after class.
  • Student continues lesson with class from the refocus area.
* **Move away** from classmates – Same as above and
  • Make parent contact.
  • Tell parents and student a Team Conference will be held upon his next referral.

OR

* **Move away** from classmates – Same as above and
  • Team Conference to problem-solve with student.
  • Tell student and parents a Parent Conference is next

OR

* **Send to buddy**
  • Send with assignment.
  • Have a Parent Conference/Contact (if possible).
  • Have student show parent his goals & action steps.
  • Have Teammates/Assistant Principal in meeting, if possible, if parent won't/can't attend, have meeting with student only. Assistant Principal tells parent and/or student what steps the office will take (In-School Suspension, Saturday School, Alternative School, Boot Camp, Juvenile Justice System, Out-of-School Suspension, etc.) if behavior continues.
* **Office Referral**

Learning Choices
Special Classes

Create Your Hierarchy

(Art, Music, P.E., Library, Computer)
(K-12 – Can start fresh each time because of recordkeeping)

- **Preminder/Cue** – When possible

- **Redirect** – Give as many as you have the patience to give

- **Move Away** from Classmates –
  Short time away from activity.
  If student says HOW he is going to refocus back to goal, allow return to activity.

- **Move Away** from Classmates – Activity is forfeited for remainder of class period.
  Student writes refocus form (Grades 2-12).
  To be able to participate in next session with this teacher it must be completed.
  Finished form may be given to teacher that class period. If not done, student takes it with him to complete.
  If lost, next class period student works on it and problem-solves with teacher before being allowed to participate again

- **Office Referral** – If student gets disruptive after being moved from other students, send to office referral area.

- After two total forfeitures of class activity, definitely contact parents.

- After three, request a parent conference.

Learning Choices - The DETAILED Picture

More Options to Use in Your Hierarchy

These can be discussed with students and numbered 1, 2, 3.
The next time student acts out, #1 occurs, then #2, then #3.

- ❑ Refocus Time in the Classroom-- ________ Minutes Each Time
- ❑ Loss or Partial Loss of Recess
- ❑ After-School Detention in Your Classroom ________ Days
- ❑ Writing a Plan to Change Behavior
- ❑ Filling Out Any of the Forms in this Book
- ❑ Writing an Apology to Victim
- ❑ Teacher/Student Call to Parents at Home or Work
- ❑ Parent Conference
- ❑ What Ideas Do You Have?
- ❑ ________________________________
- ❑ ________________________________
- ❑ Send to Another Teacher's Classroom
- ❑ Parent Shadows Student During Critical Times of Day
- ❑ Loss of Privilege
- ❑ Permanently Change Student's Seat
- ❑ Problem-Solving Conference with Teacher/Team
- ❑ Video Tape Student's Behavior for Parents
- ❑ Audio Tape Student's Outbursts
- ❑ Saturday School
- ❑ ________________________________
- ❑ ________________________________

Restitution Sheet

This is to be used when a student has violated the rights of an individual(s) or damaged school property.

Name ____________________________ Parent's Name(s) ________________________

Student Signs ____________________ Parent Signs____________________________

Today's Date ___________ Number where parent can be reached____________________

What happened was: (write on the back, if needed)

____

____

____

____

Because of what I did, how did it hurt another person?

____

____

____

Did it damage any property? How?

____

____

____

What restitution am I going to make?

____

____

____

What I could have done differently was:

____

____

____

www.dianaday.com • 972-278-7773

Acting Out or Taking Action

Directions: Read each, deciding whether the person was **Acting Out or Taking Action**. Answer all questions.

1. A student comes to your school. He has a bad reputation for being a tough kid who likes to cause trouble. Some of your friends think he's cool and funny. They encourage him to cause trouble in the younger teachers' classrooms. Some of your friends are hanging out with this student.
   A. The new student is ____ .
   B. Your friends are starting to ____.
   C. What are you going to do? ____.

2. One of your teachers is having a hard time controlling the class. The teacher starts the class being nice but as students get worse, she yells and writes referrals. Your friends tell you they think it's funny when she gets angry so they try to get her angry on purpose.
   A. Your friends are ____ .
   B. The teacher is ____
   C. What can you do to help this situation? ______________________________ .
   D. What could the teacher do to make things better? ____________________.

3. Writing has always been hard for you. You just don't know what to say on your papers. Your teacher has offered help after school but that's not cool.
   A. You are ____ .
   B. The teacher is ____ .
   C. What can you do better? ____.

4. Your parents are visiting relatives for the weekend. You begged not to have to go. They made you promise that no one would come inside the house. Your friends are begging to come over, saying your parents will never know.
   A. Your friends are ____ .
   B. Your parents expect you to ____.
   C. What will you tell your friends? ____.

5. A student in the cafeteria drops $5.00 on the floor. No one sees this but you. This student can afford to lose $5.00. You could use the money. The other student asks if anyone found $5.00. He asks you, too.
   A. The other student is ____ .
   B. You decide to ____ .
   C. Therefore, you are ____.

A Technique Called "Buddy Room"

Sending to a Well-Managed Classroom

Often a student's behavior is not so critical that he needs to be sent to the office. However, because of repetitive misbehavior, he may need to be removed from the classroom. Sending to a **"Buddy Room"** is a great solution. The student may be successfully pushing your buttons, but may not be so brave as to manipulate your buddy-teacher.

The use of **"Buddy Room,"** gives you time to take a breath, unwind emotionally and mentally prepare to have a refocus-back-to-goals meeting for 30 seconds when he returns.

"The use of 'Buddy Room' gives you time to take a breath..."

For some reason, no one wants to go to Mr. Igor's 6th grade class as a Buddy Room.

"I'm Sending Over A Sweetie!"

- It is not to be used to humiliate the student
- The buddy classroom can be 1-2 grade levels up or down (K-6). Secondary goes to a partner in the same hallway & the teacher watches him enter.
- Send to well-managed classroom.
- Keep your buddy's schedule so you do not send when no one is there.

- Student remains for a pre-determined time (usually 30 minutes or until your class is over).
- Student takes a pre-made packet of work (K-2) or work that would have been done in class (3-12).
- Student can also do a Refocus sheet.
- Buddy sends the student back with an escort, if needed, (K-6) and note about his behavior.

"This technique is extremely effective when used consistently through all the steps."

If student acts out in Buddy's class, Buddy notifies student that 30 additional minutes will be served and notifies sending teacher

If student acts out a second time, same occurs

If student acts out a third time, Buddy sends student to the office. Student can be placed in In-School Suspension (see ICU page 113) if it exists. Parents need to be called at work and told: "Two teachers cannot teach; fifty students cannot learn. Come pick up your child." Your administration will need to take this action.

Remember educators, we are not a babysitting service.

Buddy Forms

Student: Miranda Wrights — Sending Teacher: Reed M. N. Weep — Date: 9/19 — Time Out: 1:10p

☐ End of Class — Behavior: Yelled loudly, "Fanny is fat and stinky!"

☑ 30 Minutes

- - - - - - - - - - - - - - - - - - - -

Time In: 1:11p — Buddy Teacher: James Hardley Sweats — Time Out: 1:41p

☑ Acceptable: Cooperative, did work after I read her her rights.

☐ 30 Minutes

☐ Plus 30

☐ Admin. Referral

Send this form with the student.

Student: Hoss T.L. Takeover — Teacher: Rhonda Helpme — Date: 10/4 — Time Out: ______

☐ End of Class — Behavior: Refused to work, kicked desk, yelled

☑ 30

- - - - - - - - - - - - - - - - - - - -

Time In: 10:41a — Teacher: Betty Neva Sweats — Time Out: 12:11p

☐ Acceptable

☑ 30 Minutes: Very angry. Threw book at wall. Testing me.

☑ Plus 30: Calmed down after I gave +30. Did Australia Sheet.

☐ Admin. Referral

Student ______ Teacher ______ Date ______ Time Out ______

☐ End of Class — Behavior ______

☐ 30 ______

- - - - - - - - - - - - - - - - - - - -

Time In ______ Teacher ______ Time Out ______

☐ Acceptable ______

☐ 30 Minutes ______

☐ Plus 30 ______

☐ Admin. Referral ______

www.dianaday.com • 972-278-7773

Individual Coaching Unit (ICU)

Description: The ICU is an alternative classroom where students - experiencing difficulty in maintaining classroom cooperation, performing on-task behavior or following directions - are referred for "Individual Coaching."

Setting: The ICU is a regular classroom space with portable partitions/cubicles to allow for student privacy and foster the ability to focus.

Referrals: The ICU receives referrals from teachers when "Refocus Area" or "Buddy Room" has not altered behavior. Administrators may refer as part of their hierarchy of choices.

ICU - Procedures

Admittance: Students are to calm themselves and then complete one of the problem-solving forms. The referred student takes appropriate lesson materials from the referring teacher for study. Upon arrival, the ICU Coach gives the student the "3 Q's" information pack. It explains that the purpose of ICU is to complete the "3 Q's," work on the appropriate lessons, and return to class as soon as practical.

3 Q's: The "3 Q's" must be completed before the student can return to the regular classroom.

Q1: Quiet -Silence must be observed in the ICU except when using whisper voices with the ICU Coach. Movement is restricted to the student's cubicle area.

Q2: Questions must be answered before the student attempts to qualify for return to the regular classroom. The Coach may prompt the student to answer the following six questions:

1. What were you doing that caused your referral?
2. Which expectation was not met?
3. What happens to you when expectations are not met?
4. Is this what you want to happen?
5. Where at school would you rather be now?
6. What will happen if you do not meet expectations again?

Q3: Qualify to return to the classroom. The student must demonstrate a change in attitude and have a plan for what will they do differently to correct the misbehavior by completing a PACE form and discussing the form with the referring teacher. If qualified, the Coach will arrange for the student's return.

Characteristics of the ICU

Restrictive: The ICU is restrictive, but not punitive in nature. The restrictive nature, quiet and limited movement, are established to help the student regain self-control and to initiate positive goal-directed behavior as quickly as possible.

Extended: The ICU is available for students the entire school day and beyond to afford the student additional time to learn acceptable classroom behavior and to complete regular classroom assignments. The extended nature of the ICU is designed as a natural consequence of not meeting classroom expectations. The ICU day should be at least 30 minutes longer than the regular school day.

Isolation: The ICU does not allow for interaction with other students during placement except for modeling and role-playing of new behaviors. This allows the student to focus on individual goals.

Core Beliefs of the ICU

Punishment: Does nothing but drive students further away from their personal goals.

Change: The positive atmosphere in the ICU and the personal attention of the ICU Coach allows students the best opportunity to decide to change their behavior.

Motto: The motto of the ICU is "GOAL": **G**et **O**ver it **A**nd **L**earn.
Get over the past off-task behavior and start acting in your own best interest.

Theme: Each student referred is there to learn from the experience, reflect and grow internally.

Coach: The role of the Coach is always **"ER -- "Encourage Responsibility."**

Discharge from the ICU

Timing: The length of time the student spends in ICU is "self-prescribed." That is, when the "3 Q's" have been completed a teacher meeting may be requested.

Meeting: If the monitor believes the student is ready, they will schedule a meeting with the teacher or Principal.

Return: Upon return to the classroom, the student will be assigned to the "Refocus Area" for a period of time until the teacher can listen to the student's new plan.

HOLDING A TEAM CONFERENCE

"Name, thank you for leaving your _______________ class. Please take a seat. I think you know everyone here. We want your cooperation so we can help you to meet *your* goals, and we can reach ours, to teach. We are specifically concerned that _______________."

Coming together is a beginning;
Keeping together is progress;
Working together is success.
Henry Ford

1. What is it that you are trying to accomplish with this behavior?
2. Is it working?
3. Is it helping or hurting you to reach your goal of _______________.
4. What do you think will happen if you continue to do what you are doing?
5. Is there a better way to accomplish what you want?
6. If you were to write another goal today, what would it be?
7. Which of your action steps do you need to focus upon to make your goal a reality?
8. Each of us cares about you and wants you to succeed. We will meet again with you on ________ to check your progress. (Name), thank you for your cooperative attitude."

We cannot
hold a
torch to
another's
path without
brightening
our own.
Ben Sweetland

We gain what we want through
the help and support of others.
Cooperation:
To be agreeable, to be liked, to cooperate.
This contributes immeasurably to our success.
When we coordinate our efforts with the efforts of others, we
speed the way to our goals. Cooperation builds success.
Diana Day

Teacher ____________ **DOCUMENTATION** Week Of ____________

Student's Name	Monday	Tuesday	Wednesday	Thursday	Friday

Only write the names of students who refuse your redirects & are sent to Refocus, Buddy, ICU or Office.
Write the # of the expectation (rule) they violated. Record **exact** bad language.
You are able to get a conduct grade from these weekly reports.

INSTALLATION OF VISION MANAGEMENT©

SET-UP

- **Post PEDS** - inside of door
- **Learning Expectations** - front wall
- **MAPS Routines*** - front wall
- **Teacher Scripts** - back wall
- **Position Stub Cans and Paper Recycle Boxes**
- **Prepare Pride Folders, Goal Sheets, Refocus Forms**
- **Position Desks** - quick walking path

PREVENTION STRATEGIES

- **Circulate, giving private cues and redirects**
    - **Cues** - Big Eyes, Touch, Answer
    - **Redirects** -

      "You are... (what student is doing wrong)."

      "I want... (what student is expected to do)."
- **Explain Expectations** - Model and Role-play
- **Read *Goal-For-It*©*, *Day2Day*©*** daily to students
- **Introduce** the concept of goal writing with action steps
- **Use affirming gestures** to celebrate success

* ***Goal-For-It***© in the catalog at the end of this book-page 138

* ***Day2Day***© in the catalog at the end of this book-page 137

Level One — Classroom Interventions

- Change student's seat
- In-room "learning choice" (Refocus area)
- Pride Folder/Goals Sheet Talk - 2 minutes
- Hallway, Classroom Student/Teacher refocus talk - 30 seconds
- Student required to self-manage using "Refocus Sheets"
- Parent Contact

Level Two — Classroom Interventions

- Out-of-class "Learning Choice" (Buddy Room)
- Students writes refocus sheet
- Parents contacted
- Possible counselor referral
- Possible Parent/Teacher/Team meeting
- Reasons: Chronic misbehavior
  Refusal to work/uncooperative
  Mild destructive behavior

Student refuses intervention

Level Three — Teacher-Initiated Office Referral

- Teacher writes Office Disciplinary Referral
  Must be either:
  -Disruptive/Uncooperative in Buddy Room
  -Critical Misbehavior in classroom after return from Buddy Room

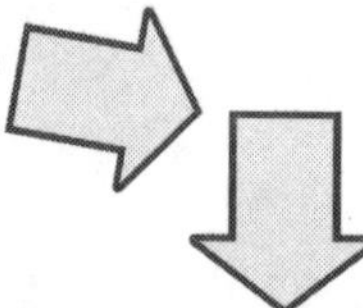

Level Three — Office Referral

- Received referral based on critical misbehavior
  Reasons:
  -Refusal/swearing at teacher
  -Fighting, hitting, screaming
  -Threats/Harassment/Intimidation
  -Inappropriate physical contact
  -Use/possession of illegal substances or items (drugs, alcohol or weapons)
  -Inappropriate attire and refusal to change
  -Destroying/Damaging property

Level Four — Administrative Action

- ICU - Intensive Care Unit
- Work on goals, restitution, new plan
- Out-of-school Suspension
- Parent contacted, short ICU for restitution sheet
- ICU until parents conference with team and administration
- Law enforcement called

www.dianaday.com • 972-278-7773

Chapter 7

It's an Inside Job: Self-Motivation

Winners Are Not Born, They Are Made

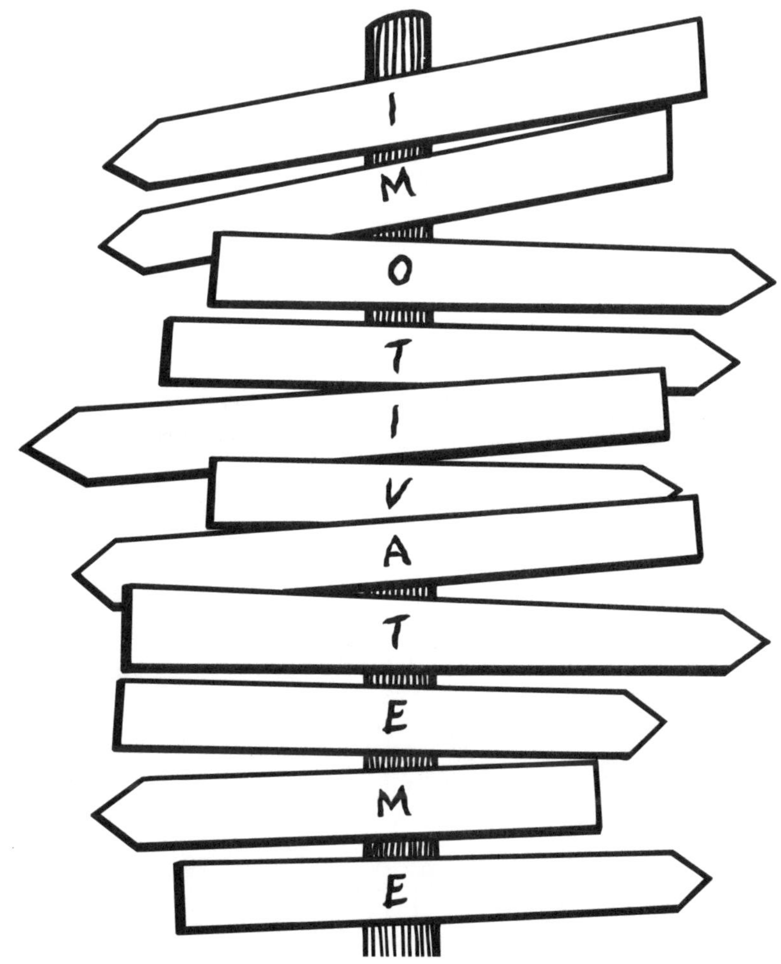

*"The visionary teacher,
looking for the best in each student,
guides the student to
envision the best
in him/herself."*

What Is a Learning Incentive?

Definition

A **"learning incentive"** is anything that would strengthen or support an action or attitude that increases learning. The term "learning incentive" is to be substituted for these old terms:

- reward
- positive consequence
- positive reinforcement.

Effective Incentives

An Effective Learning Incentive:

- Can be intrinsic or, in moderation, extrinsic
- Is something the learner chooses to motivate him/herself
- Can be designed to provide an incentive to succeed
- Can be a prize for having succeeded

Intrinsic incentives are superior *to extrinsic ones because the learner provides the stimuli to succeed and, therefore, has a greater sense of achievement when success is reached.* Students' goals might be to pass a test, learn a skill, have more friends or move to a higher grade. When students accomplish their goals and set new ones, they comprehend that their destiny is truly in their hands. They begin the lifelong realization, "if it's to be, it's up to me."

When teachers praise verbally or show positive facial expressions when learners succeed, even in small ways, it becomes a lantern that lights the path on the learners' journey to greater success. The lantern needs to be lit when students have selected the right "path" after days or weeks of poor choices. It can be lit when students reach the summit, having achieved their goal. It can even be lit when they are on level ground but are continuing to move forward.

> *"Progress is the name of the game."*

Progress is the name of the game. It is what counts. **Every person, child or adult, yearns to have someone believe in him, to provide encouragement.** Encouragement and celebration of a job well done is a requirement to aspire to greater success to share the joy of achievement.

TEMPORARY VS. PERMANENT CHANGE

The philosophy of *Vision Management©* is to encourage intrinsic incentives **generously** and extrinsic in **moderation**. Teachers certainly give extrinsic reinforcement with good intentions. But, many dole out extrinsic reinforcers for meager effort, and others, for no effort at all. Soon students are saying, "What will you give me to do it?"

We have discussed that we are to be the lantern that guides the way. That lantern represents verbal praise and encouragement. We must not hold out a sticker or candy to show the way. When teachers praise students for the positive choices and the EFFORT they've made, they are giving them increased empowerment. They are providing internal thrust that drives students to move forward under their own power. Overdosing on extrinsics, will drive students to beg for rewards, then have a performance plateau until the next reward is offered.

Although punishment, or heavy use of extrinsic rewards, can temporarily halt misbehavior, only the power of intrinsic motivation can support a permanent change of behavior. Remembering to praise takes forethought and practice. Seeking out the positive event is a new experience for some teachers. It may be our conditioning. Many parents raised their children with strong discipline, many negatives and few positives. We have the ability to break this cycle of being merely a watchdog for bad behavior by expecting the positive and recognizing it when it occurs.

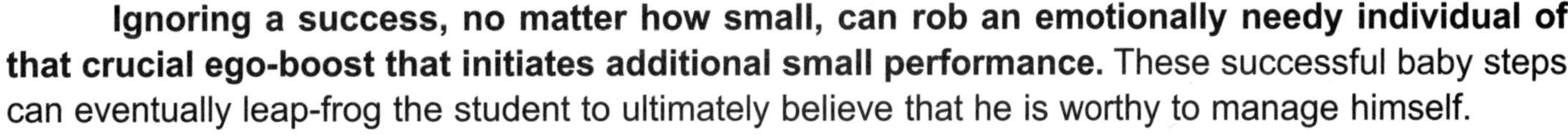

It has been said:

IT TAKES 20 POSITIVES TO OFFSET ONE NEGATIVE COMMENT OR EXPERIENCE

Ignoring a success, no matter how small, can rob an emotionally needy individual of that crucial ego-boost that initiates additional small performance. These successful baby steps can eventually leap-frog the student to ultimately believe that he is worthy to manage himself.

Self-motivation and self-management can be instilled in children even in lower primary grades by using *Vision Management©*. Upon entering secondary school, these students excel over students who have been managed through the use of punishment and rewards.

> *"...student-driven accomplishments build self-esteem..."*

Student-driven accomplishment builds self-esteem, increases self-worth and multiplies motivation exponentially.

How to Prepare for True Self-Management

"Focus on the Student's Goal, Not the Student's Misbehavior."

Students, of any age, are capable of telling, drawing or writing what it is that they desire, if nothing could stop them. Some elect to name an academic, behavior or personal desire. And, some are so excited, they name a desire for each category. These desires are their **"goals."**

We also know that merely stating a goal, does not make it happen. It is the accuracy of the action steps, and the drive to consistently stick with them that ultimately leads students to success. Because so few adults write personal goals to focus upon a "life plan," few children have been exposed to the wonders of knowing that their destiny lies in the actions they do or do not perform.

> *"...merely stating a goal does not make it happen..."*

When teachers conference with students, the most important piece of documentation is the students' Goal Sheet or Pride Folder. If a student does not have one, explain what it is and ask him to thoughtfully write one. The purpose of the conference is not to hammer students about misbehavior but to refocus them back to their true desire...their goal. **Once they return to their belief that their desired goal is more important to them than acting out, they will change their actions, or misbehavior!**

The essence of a "problem-solving" conference is to focus upon whether the action, or lack of action by the student, contributed to or hindered the progress towards his desire...or goal. This can be discussed in as much detail as time allows. Focusing on the misdeed with the teacher behaving in an authoritarian, parental, permissive or monitor management style, is not going to encourage change.

www.dianaday.com • 972-278-7773

How to Be the Messenger for Change

Building Motivation from Within

When a sincere, caring person helps students to see where they are headed as a result of these excellent or poor choices, most students comprehend the power they have to choose the way they wish to lead their lives. They can take the high road or the low road.

> ***"Only your students can make this decision and they must be motivated from within."***

Only your students can make this decision and they must be motivated from within. Almost all students will make the decision to move from misbehavior to behavior that positively impacts their desires…or goals.

What's the P.A.C.E. Form?

On the following pages, The PACE Form will be introduced. It will be a concrete measure to determine what actions create change.

People whose belief system is that children should be punished into goodness will find that their methods work only as long as the punisher holds the stick. Punishment, or fear of it, is a temporary "solution," at best. It has also been shown that highly stressful environments reduce the ability of students to retain information in short-term memory.

Teachers have enormous power to change students' lives for the better. By using the PACE form, it becomes clear to students that what they did five minutes ago impacted their lives. What they change in the next five minutes can get them back on-track.

WANT CHANGE? USE THE PACE FORM

SELF-ASSESSMENT - THE BEST ASSESSMENT

P.A.C.E. stands for Planned Action & Commitment Everyday. It provides an assessment tool for students to reflect upon their progress toward their goals.

"It is important that the action steps be very specific..."

The students write their goal at the top. This can be copied from their Goal Sheet. The action steps are listed. It is important that these action steps be very specific and clear. Ask students to tell you how each of their action steps strengthens the possibility of successfully reaching their goal.

Is it worth the effort? If you have continued to read to this chapter, you believe it is.

SELF-ASSESSMENT TO SELF-AWARENESS

Everyday, either the entire class, or the student who needs the most reorganizing and support, self-assesses performance of each action step by giving it a numerical score. Without much effort, students will reach a self-awareness level that guides them to know what actions are taking them towards or away from their goal.

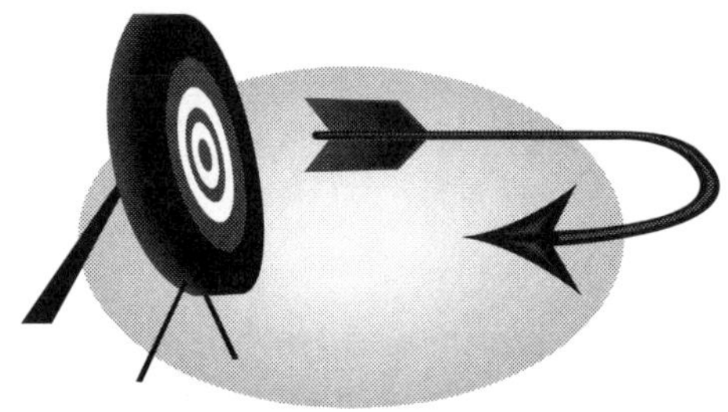

It takes a caring adult, who has a relationship with these students to initiate problem-solving and discussion about what, how, and when changes need to be made. If the student lives in an environment where family members have negative attitudes, low aspirations, or do not even take time to interact with the their child, the teacher will be the last bastion of support, care and hope.

PACE

Planned Action & Commitment Everyday

Name ____________
Date ____________

My Goal ______________________________

Specific Action Steps	Monday	Tuesday	Wednesday	Thursday	Friday	
My Daily Total →						

Self-Scoring Key

Evaluating My Action Steps	My Daily Total
5 = I did my very best today.	32-35 = I did my very best today.
4 = I really came close to doing my best.	28-31 = I really came close to doing my best.
3 = I could have done better.	20-27 = I could have done better.
2 = I could have done a lot better.	10-19 = I could have done a lot better.
1 = I didn't do very well today.	Under 9 = Are my action steps realistic?

Guidelines for Building Self-Esteem

- Use verbal encouragement continuously. (Remember, it takes 20 positives to offset one careless negative comment.)

- Do not overuse extrinsic reinforcement. Eventually, students expect a reward for any effort and the goodies become ineffective.

- Have criteria established for how and why you'll distribute tangible rewards.

"Do not overuse extrinsic reinforcement."

- Smile or speak to every student every day. Preferably call them by name.

- Have some students use the PACE form daily so they can see progress towards goals.

"Remember to PACE yourself."

- Enlist support from the class to encourage and support one another.

- Remind or set a time weekly for students to add paperwork they're proud of to their PRIDE folders.

Pigskin Review

When a review is needed, it often seems the only person answering the questions from the review is the teacher. A great learning incentive for positive behavior is to challenge the students to a Pigskin Review. If the students have shown cooperation with one another, they have earned the special review.

The day before the review, give students index cards on which to write questions with answers that they believe will be on an exam. The day of the review draw a football field on the chalkboard or create an overlay using page 128. Divide the class into two teams and flip a coin to see which team receives the ball. Set the timer for a specified period of time.

Using the students' index cards, ask each team member in turn a question. Ten yards are earned for each correct answer.

Other rules are:

Fumble - Player gives wrong answer. Other team takes over play and is asked same question.

Ineligible Receiver - Wrong player on team gives answer. Other team takes over play and is asked a new question.

Offside - Someone on the other team answers out of turn. Team with ball gets an extra 10 yards and is asked a new question.

Punt - When the ball is fumbled 3 consecutive times, say, "Punt." The first person from either team to raise his/her hand and give the correct answer earns 10 yards and a new question.

For the point after the touchdown, you may ask a question from your personal set of index card questions. If the team wants to go for 3 points, the question can be more difficult.

Put a time limit on play. The team with the most points wins when the timer goes off.

FOOTBALL FIELD

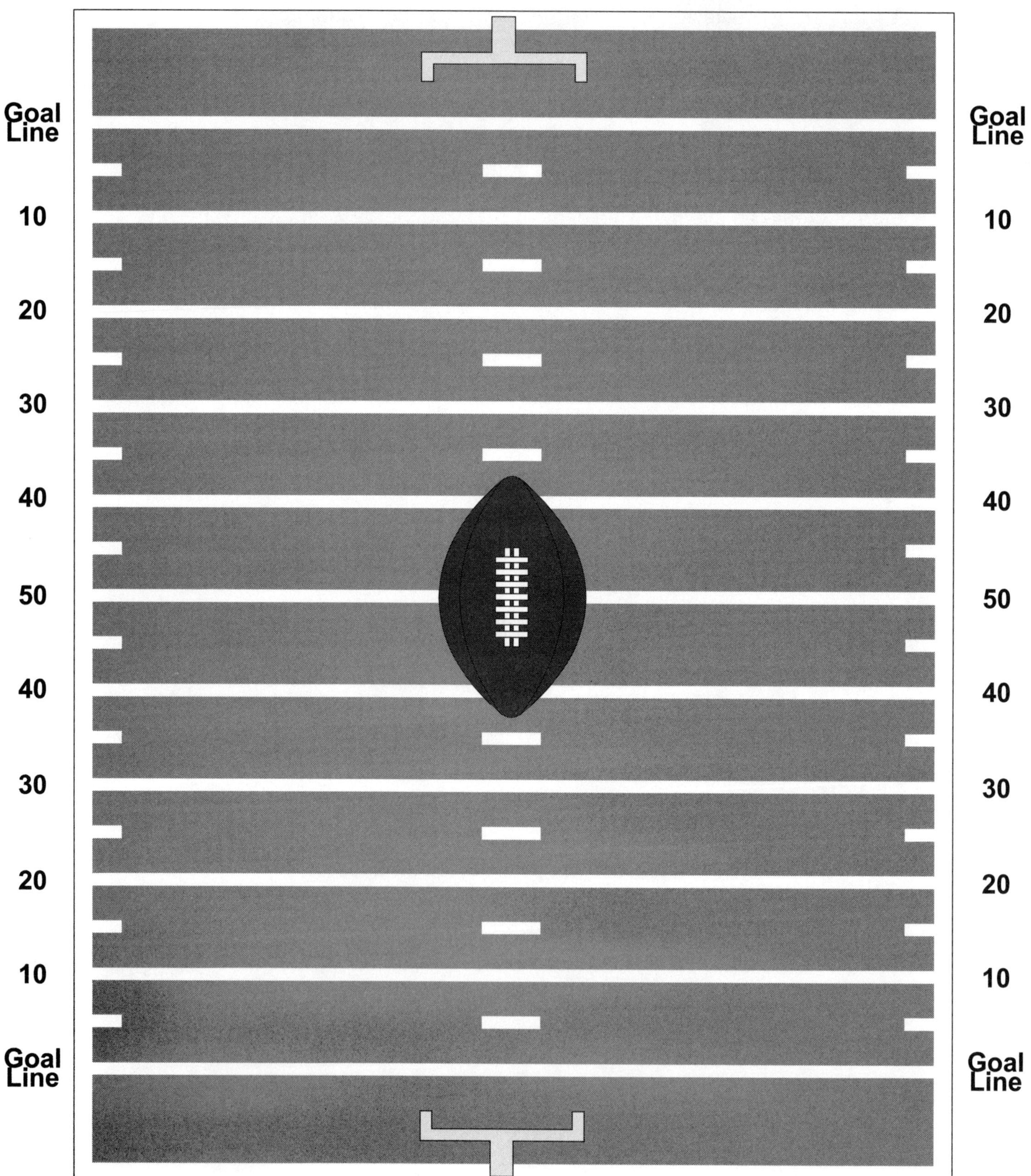

Summary of Vision Theory©

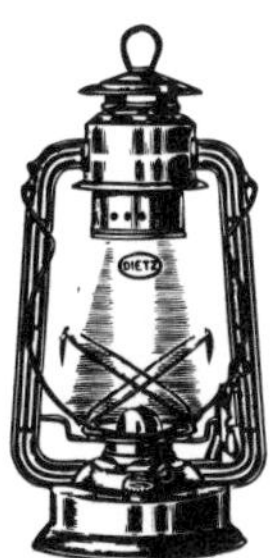

Vision Theory© is the underlying concept from which *Vision Management©* evolved. It is a behavior philosophy that believes all action is initiated by **internal belief** rather than **external stimulus**. To change behavior, we first need to change the **belief** prompting the behavior.

Critical core beliefs of Vision Theory© include:

- Discipline must not be punishment, rather, it is the ability to maintain focus while working toward a **self-set goal**.
- Punishment does nothing but punish. Refocusing students on their goals serves a much higher purpose. The **"ultimate punishment"** is not to achieve your potential.
- Brain research has shown that even **threatening** punishment does nothing but stimulate the undesirable behavior.
- Consequences for **"not-in-my-own-best-interest"** behavior are to remind, redirect, and refocus students back to the action steps necessary to take them closer to their goals.
- We cannot **make** anyone do anything. We can only influence or inspire. Cooperation is much stronger and longer lasting than coercion.
- We are motivated by our **needs**: survival, love, fun, power and freedom. With maturation, the ultimate need is to identify and attain one's **self-ideal**.
- People do react to external "**should's**," but an internal **"I take responsibility"** is much more powerful.
- Each individual is **special and unique** and has a purpose for his/her life.
- **Behavior is best influenced** when a school's educational mission is integrated with its character-building mission.
- For a campus to succeed, there must be **commitment, cooperation and common purpose** established, agreed and acted upon, consistently by the adults in charge.
- A **Campus Covenant** establishes the purpose, expectations, standards and policies that guide the school. Strong leadership is desirable, but alone cannot replace such an agreement.
- The **key to an effective behavior management plan** is the consistent, objective and kind application of expectations (rules) with learning choices (consequences). These components must be understood and acceptable to all concerned with the student's welfare. Any lowering of these standards creates a new lowest common denominator standard. This new LCD standard can be set by any educator who accepts, ignores, tolerates or fails to recognize the substandard behavior. Only when standards are established, maintained and enforced will schools once again become safe, inviting and invigorating climates for learning. All policies, standards and expectations should be "zero tolerance."
- We cannot control others. They might force us to try to control them, **or** they can learn to control themselves.

Vision Theory

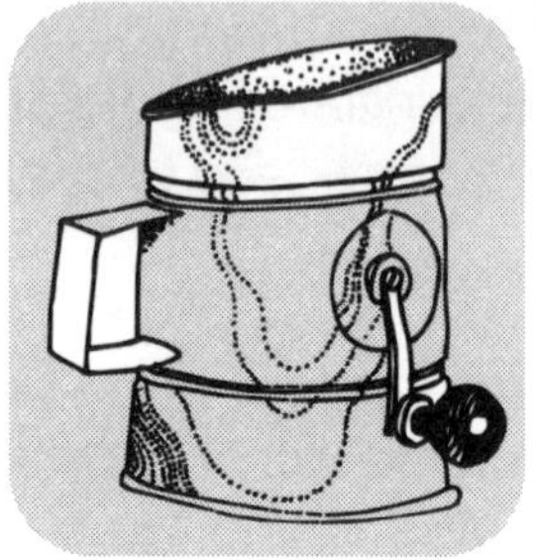

1.

2.

3.

4.

5.

Having slowly and thoughtfully processed each critical belief of the Summary:

1. Go back through your book matching concrete techniques to the Vision Theory©.

2. Commit to 5 changes you will make to improve not only your students, but also you yourself.

3. Reread the Vision Theory© philosophy frequently to recommit yourself to a modern way of interacting with others.

Thank you for either participating in a live program or doing a self-study.

"Together we make a better world by guiding young people to imagine, believe in, and experience their ultimate potential to do the same."

Diana Day

My Action Plan

Vision Management©

_______ ☐ 1. Create your Professional Educator Dedication Statement (PEDS) (pages 24-28).

_______ ☐ 2. Write PEDS on poster and attach to a front bulletin board or inside of door at eye-level.

_______ ☐ 3. Reproduce Student Dedication Statement Sheets (page 29).

_______ ☐ 4. Reproduce Student Goal Worksheets (page 33 & 41).

_______ ☐ 5. Plan interesting lessons to teach how to write a goal, write a student dedication statement and to explain your classroom management plan.

_______ ☐ 6. Reproduce parent support letter (pages 66-67) and Classroom Management Plan letter for parents (pages 81-82).

_______ ☐ 7. Reproduce copies of forms you plan to use:

Your PEDS (pages 24-26)
Student Dedication Statement (pg. 42)
Student Goal Worksheets (pages 47-52)
Getting Back On Track (pg. 54)
Spiral Up/Spiral Down (pg. 55)
Want More Friends? (pg. 56)
Six Habits of Successful Students (pg. 57)
4-D Solution (pg. 58)
Top 10 Reasons (pg. 59)
3...2...1 Blastoff (pg. 60)
Driver's Seat (pg. 62)
Pre-School/K Expectations (pg. 75)
Classroom Expectations Gr. 1/12 (pg. 76)
Refocus Sheet (pg. 98)
Pre K/K Goal Sheet (pg. 99)
Restitution Sheet (pg. 108)
Documentation Form (pg. 77)
Buddy Forms (pg. 112)
Documentation (pg. 116)
PACE Form (pg. 125)

_______ ☐ 8. Obtain student PRIDE Folders and organize to use (35-37).

_______ ☐ 9. Reproduce and laminate goals Sheet Script (40).

_______ ☐ 10. Take a deep breath and visualize your personal confidence & ability.

"Share What You Love"

Yes, we all are teachers
teaching all the time.
Yes, we all are students
learning line by line.

Why be a teacher
at times we do ask?
To share what we love
make good on the past.

First we teach ourselves
what we most need to learn.
Then we teach others
when it becomes their turn.

With each and every lesson
each day we've got to prove
We can get their attention
we can get in their groove.

We teach best with passion
our purposes displayed.
Keep focused on your goals
don't ever be dismayed.

It's always an uphill battle
for the minds of the very young.
But teachers are missionaries
their job just begun.

The baby boomers listened
to their parents few firm words,
But the X Generation
thinks we're just a bunch of nerds.

No reason to listen
no reason they say.
Our passion must flourish
to still save the day.

From ABC to MTV
from Beaver Cleaver to Brittany Spears.
It seems like time eternal
instead of fifty years.

From drive-ins to drive -bys
from the Beatles to KISS
What's happened to our nation?
When did we begin to miss?

We tried authoritarian.
Tried spare the rod and spoil the child.
And, then, we tried permissiveness
and let the kids run wild.

We tried "parental judgmental"
to stop the downward trend.
And finally we became monitors
keeping score to the very end.

But today there's only one way:
Get "vision" from up above!
Be firm, be fair and always care.
Don't teach, share what you love!

Rick Pehrson

Be the Best You Can Be!

Change your thinking; change your future.
You can accomplish all that your mind can embrace.

HAPPINESS

Begin today!
If nothing could stop you, what would you want to do or become?
It must be good for you and not hurt other people

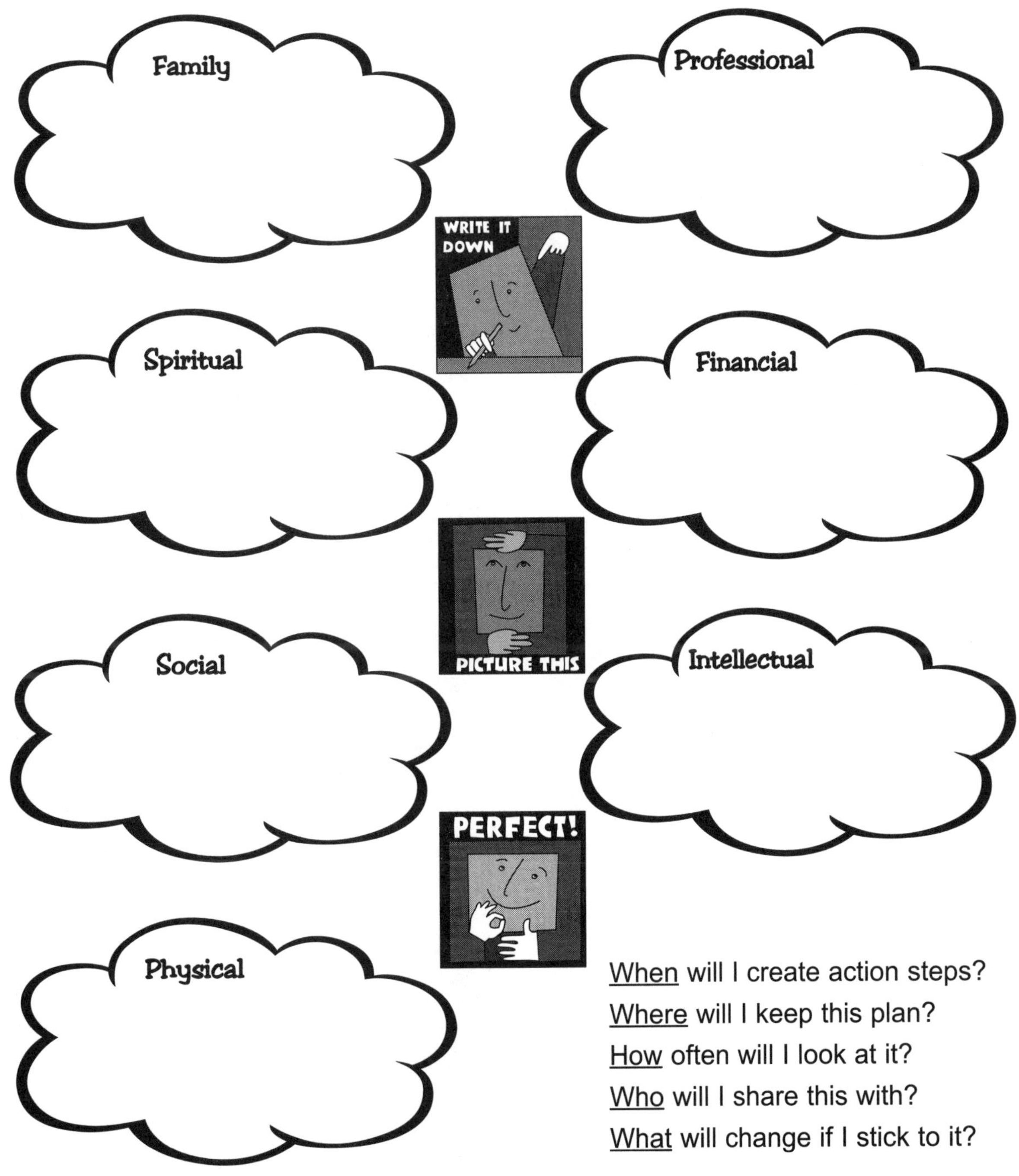

<u>When</u> will I create action steps?
<u>Where</u> will I keep this plan?
<u>How</u> often will I look at it?
<u>Who</u> will I share this with?
<u>What</u> will change if I stick to it?

PLAN
For the Future

...Check out the catalog!
Turn "Before"
into "After"

Mission Statement:

Our mission is to deliver exemplary discipline management training and unique support materials to sustain positive behavior by students at school and at home.

"Give students discipline and you've made ***your day*** *better.*
Teach students self-discipline and you've made ***their lives*** *better."*

Vision Management©

Educators K-12, Counselors, Spec. Education, New Teachers

- 96-Page Text Detailing How To Set-Up a Discipline Management Plan
- Supplies Discipline Link Missing From Character-Building Programs
- Features Student Self-Management, Self-Assessment With Many Reproducible Pages
- Used Campuswide, Has Decreased Office Referrals 49-89%

$19.95

Challenging Students©

Educators K-12, Counselors, Spec. Education, New Teachers

- 80-Page Text Unlocks The Mystery of the "Hard-to-Manage"
- Be a Successful Teacher With Unmotivated, Demanding and Difficult Students
- Steps to Avoid Being Hooked Into a Confrontation
- How To Reverse Repeated Misbehavior
- Master The "7 Steps to Teach a New Behavior"

Pencil Holder

Imprinted with "Is your Vision focused on your goals?" A great start-the-year or appreciation gift for staff! Holds any pen or pencil. White/royal blue. Documentation at your fingertips!

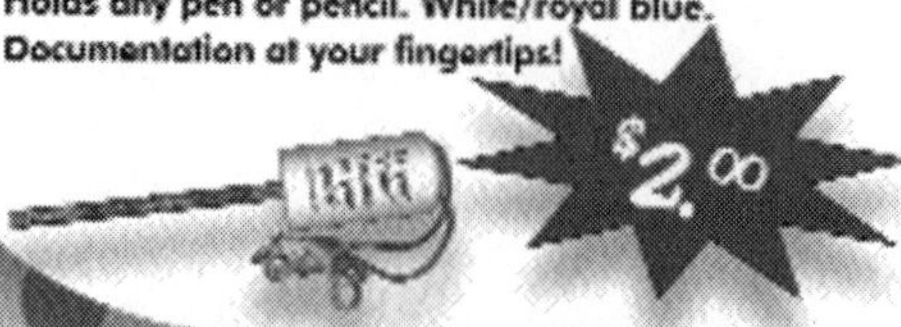

Intro to Vision Management© Audio Tape

Helpful discipline management reminders for new teachers to listen to on the way to school. Great daily reminders for daily success!

Posters

Dedication Poster - (blue): For Teacher Commitment to Help Students Succeed

Management Plan - (yellow): Preprinted Behavior Management Plan

Desktop Mentor©

Educators K-12, Spec. Education, New Teachers

72 Answers to The Most-Asked Questions in Behavior Management in an Easy-Reference Spiral Book.

- How To Set-Up an Effective Discipline Management System
- Handling Back-Talk, Disputes, Incomplete Work
- Stopping Disrespect, Tattling, Bullying
- Responses for Refusal, Arguments between Students

An indispensable tool for new and veteran teachers alike!

Say, "I am going to teach you an experiment about vibration. Everyone take your hand and place four fingers...not just your fingertips, your fingers... on your throat. When I give the signal, say your name aloud 2 times. Feel the vibration your vocal cords make on your fingers! How many of you felt the vibration? Vibration means you were NOT whispering."

"This time , when I give the signal, say your name so only your work partner can hear it...a whisper. You will NOT feel any vibrations on your fingers if your are whispering. CONGRATULATIONS, you have just learned how to whisper!"

13. WHISPER VOICE: HOW TO TEACH IT

Day 2 Day© Motivational Messages

Best Seller!

Principals, Educators K-8, Counselors, Spec. Education, New Teachers

One-Minute Intercom Messages that Inspire

- 180 Interactive, Often Humorous, Always Thought-Provoking Announcements
- Weekly Themes With Word-of-The-Week
- Focus Students and Teachers on Self-Improvement
- Build Character, Values, Manners, Respect and Teamwork by Using as 2-5 Minute Lessons

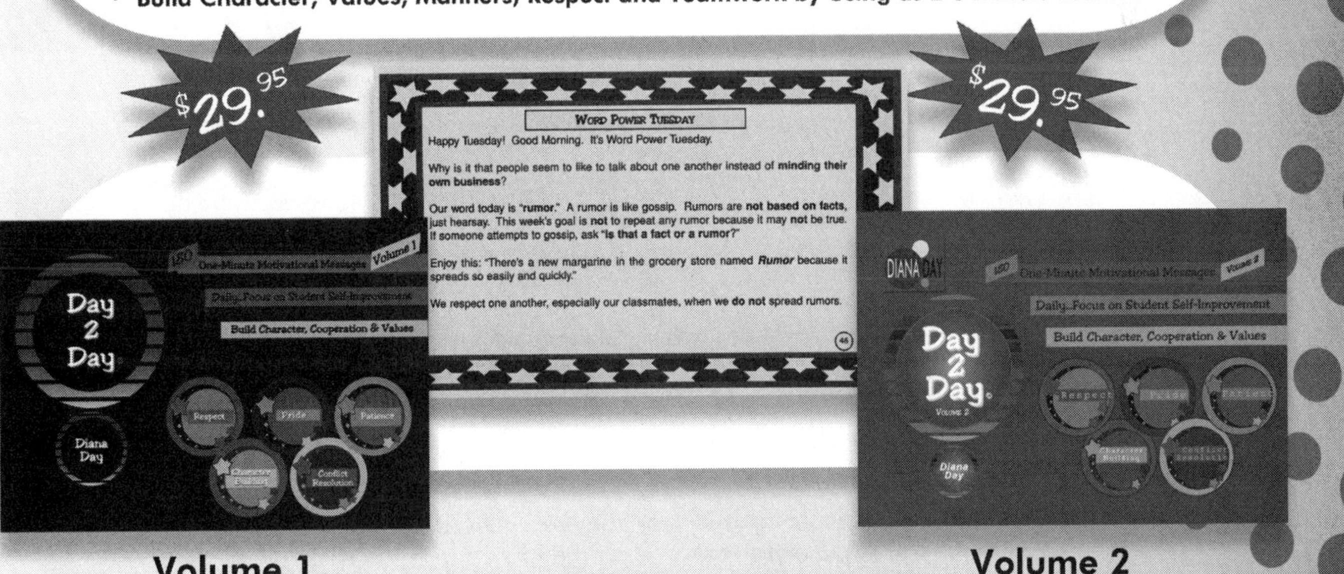

Volume 1

Volume 2

Order Today 972•278•7773 24-hour Fax 972•278•8584

Goal For It!© K-4

Educators K-4, Counselors, Spec. Education

- 39 Powerful Lessons That Establish a Complete Discipline System
- Stories and Lessons Teach Why There Are Rules and Consequences
- Plus, Celebrating Success, Goal-Setting, Never Giving Up, Handling Bullies, Resolving Conflict, How To Think Before You Act
- Book Comes With 2 Plush Puppets

$19.95

Goal For It!© 5-12

Educators 5-12, Counselors, Spec. Education

Perfect book for ADVISORY or Health classes where teachers value quick, meaningful hero stories that motivate and inspire, complete with questions/answers and short activity.

Teaches necessity of rules, boundaries, having good character, self-motivation, goal-setting, never giving up, overcoming hardship, recognizing opportunity and believing in oneself.

$14.95

Visions Character-Building Binder©

Educators K-8, Counselors

A Year of Weekly Lessons for K-3 and 4-8 That Teach: Putting Out Effort, Respectfulness, Recognizing Opportunities, Patience, Celebrating Success, Being Responsible

- 72 Lessons (36 for K-3 and 36 for 4-8) for How To Goal-Set & Improve Character & Respectfulness
- Interactive, Fun Lessons With Overlay Masters & Worksheets
  - Buy One Binder and Get School Site License to Reproduce for Each Classroom
  - 4 Imprinted, Sectional Dividers for Your Reproduced Binders are Sold Separately

911 For Parents© Live Performance

Sanity-Saving Skills to Take The Stress Out of Discipline at Home

Give parents a lifelong gift of training, taking frustration and stress out of discipline, creating calm, positive and meaningful interactions at home.

School groups, churches, hospitals and industry have sponsored the "911 for Parents" program for over 250,000 parents. Can be scheduled in any 2-3 hour time block.

We create your advertising masters and provide you, free-of-charge, "Getting Parents To Attend the '911 for Parents' Program." Call for information about this vital program.

2-3 hr. Live Performance

Diana with a parent, role-playing his son!

911 For Parents© Video Training Kit

Teachers & counselors use this video presentation, filmed with a live audience, to teach parents how to better manage their children. Create consistent discipline between home & school. Get parent support using four 30-minute, fast-paced videos.

Best Seller!

Includes 4 Videos, 62-Page Leader's Guide and Parent Hand-Outs & Overlays in English & Spanish.

$329.95

911 For Parents© Video-Viewing Set

The perfect tool to lend to all parents struggling with misbehaving children. Includes four 30-minute videos filled with humorous examples & valuable information in a sturdy storage case.

Vision Management® Workshop

Educators K-12, Counselors, Spec. Education, Aides, Clerks

How To Achieve Student Self-Management

- Creates Competence, Cooperation & Consistency With All Staff Campuswide
- Increases On-Task Behavior and Improves Test Scores
- Supplies Discipline Link Missing From Character-Building Programs
- Teaches Student Self-Management and Self-Assessment
- Used Campuswide, Has Decreased Office Referrals 49-89%
- Includes a 96-Page Text Detailing How To Set-Up a Discipline Management Plan, a Management Plan Poster and a Teacher Dedication Poster

7 hr. Live Performance

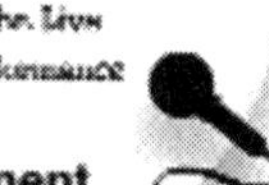

Enhance The Vision® Workshop

Educators K-12, Counselors, Spec. Education, Aides, Clerks

Tools To Regain Classroom Control

- Establish Effective Classroom Procedures That Prevent Problems Before They Begin
- Successful Strategies With Practice to Use With Students Who Refuse, Disrupt and Disrespect
- End Student Back-Talk, Disputes Between Students and Arguments With Teachers

7 hr. Live Performance

Challenging Students® Workshop

Educators K-12, Counselors, Spec. Education, Aides, Clerks

Unlocking The Mystery of Hard-to-Manage Kids

- How to Refocus & Manage Difficult, Distracted and Troubled Students
- Be a Successful Teacher With Unmotivated, Demanding and Difficult Students
- Steps to Avoid Being Hooked Into a Confrontation
- How to Reverse Repeated Misbehavior
- Master the "7 Steps to Teach a New Behavior"
- Includes 80-Page Text That Will Help Students Succeed

7 hr. Live Performance

Effective Parent Conferences® Workshop

Educators K-12, Counselors, Spec. Education, Aides, Clerks

Improve Student Behavior Through Conferencing, Calling and Communicating

- Unique Strategies to Conference, Call and Communicate With Uncooperative Parents
- Powerful Words That Prompt Cooperation
- Useful Scripts to Use for Challenging Situations

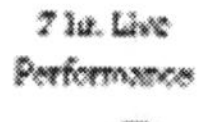

911 For Bus Drivers© Workshop

Behavior Management Training for Transportation Specialists

A Fun and Informative 2-1/2 - 3 Hour Program That Will:

- Create a Positive Climate, Competence and Consistency in Behavior Management with Drivers
- Lower Turnover Rate of Drivers
- Reduce Vandalism to Buses
- Avoid Escalating Confrontations

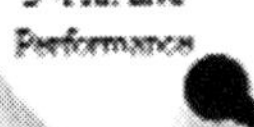

3-4 hr. Live Performance

911© For Lunch Monitors Workshop

Success Strategies for Managing Your Cafeteria

A Detailed, Informative 3-hour Session That:

- Organizes Your Cafeteria for Success
- Instills Confidence, Competence and Consistency
- Creates an Orderly, Quite Environment

3 hr. Live Performance

Administrative Leadership Series©

Train your anagement team or School Board with 3 - 6 hour training at your site or on retreat.

- "How To Handle Discipline As An Administrative Team©"
- "The 10 Most Common Mistakes That Leaders Make©"
- "Team Vision©: How to Get Cooperation, Better Communication and Collaboration From Uncooperative People"

3-6 hr. Live Performance

Workshop Details

Length: 1/2 to full-day programs

Materials: Complete with bound, interactive workbooks or packets

Cost: Call today for a quote!

Get a FREE Day2Day© Volume 1 when you schedule your workshop & say "discipline management made easy"!

For More Information

about any of these dynamic workshops, or to order materials, contact us TODAY!

Diana Day Training Center
P.O. Box 472283
Garland, Texas 75047-2283
972.278.7773 · fax 972.278.8584
goals@dianaday.com · www.dianaday.com

"New Teacher" Behavior Management Kits

Staff Developers, Spec. Education, Educators K-12, Administrators

What is the #1 Reason New Teachers Struggle?

1. LACK OF AN EFFECTIVE MANAGEMENT PLAN
2. Do Not Know What to Say or Do When Students Refuse or Disrespect
3. Do Not Have a Tool In-Hand to Guide Them Step-by-Step Through The Management Process

The Solution: Provide them with 6 Essential Tools for Success

K-12

K-12

K-4

5-12

K-12

as low as $39.50

It's easy as 1...2...3

How to Get a FREE Live Presentation or Phone Consultation

1. **Call us for a "New Teacher Kit" Info Guide**
2. **Place a Qualifying Order for "NEW TEACHER" BEHAVIOR MANAGEMENT KITS**
3. **Schedule Your FREE Services -- a $350 to $1,250 value**
   - A Two-Hour Phone Consultation With Your Administrative Team, Site-Based Committee and All Teachers With "NEW TEACHER" BEHAVIOR MANAGEMENT KITS

     -OR-
   - A Half-Day Live Presentation for all Teachers Receiving The "NEW TEACHER" BEHAVIOR MANAGEMENT KITS (Expenses Additional)

About Diana

Diana Day, a native of St Louis, Missouri, presently lives in Dallas, Texas. She has been a leader in the field of behavior management for 30 years. Diana has personally trained over one half million teachers, 250,000 parents and 15,000 bus drivers and lunchroom monitors! Her humorous and insightful keynotes have been heard by school boards, principals and teachers internationally.

Diana's teaching career has included every grade at elementary and secondary levels. She has taught Special Education and severely emotionally disturbed adolescents in a psychiatric hospital. Diana has taught at 8 major U.S. universities. She has written seventeen books and innumerable magazine articles, and is a sought-after speaker around the world.

She has always had a visionary, entrepreneurial spirit. At the young age of 22, she received an award from General Motors for the writing & direction of the "Outstanding Product Film of the Year." At age 24, Diana was assistant to the president of Carroll Shelby Racing, the largest auto racing company in America. By the age of 34, she was founder of AutoMark, an auto accessories company, Permanent Press Inc. and was also teaching and writing.

Former President Clinton awarded Diana the prestigious "Arkansas Traveler" award - originally bestowed upon Charles Lindbergh - for her contribution to education.

DIANA DAY TRAINING PRODUCTS

discipline management made easy

P.O. Box 472283 • Garland, TX 75047-2283
972-278-7773 • fax 972-278-8584
goals@dianaday.com • www.dianaday.com

Page #	Item		Item #	Price	Quantity	Amount
2	*Vision Management©* Text - 144 pgs.	NEW!	DD1001	$ 24.95		
2	*Challenging Students©* Text	NEW!	DD1002	$ 19.95		
2	Pencil Holder		DD1003	$ 2.00		
2	*Intro to Vision Management©* Audio Tape		DD1004	$ 9.95		
2	Poster - Classroom Dedication (blue)		DD1005	$ 2.25		
2	Poster - Management Plan (yellow)		DD1006	$ 2.25		
3	*Desktop Mentor©* (72 Scripted answers)	NEW!	DD1007	$ 19.95		
3	*Day 2 Day©* Volume 1		DD1008	$ 29.95		
3	*Day 2 Day©* Volume 2	NEW!	DD1009	$ 29.95		
4	*Goal For It! K-4©* (Includes two plush puppets)		DD1010	$ 19.95		
4	*Goal For It! 5-12©* (Advisory class, ISS book)	NEW!	DD1011	$ 14.95		
4	*VISIONS Character-Building Binder©*		DD1012	$249.95		
4	Imprinted Dividers for reproducible *VISIONS Binder©*		DD1013	$ 2.00		
5	*"911 for Parents"©* Video Training Kit (for training parents)		DD1014	$329.95		
5	*"911 for Parents"©* Video-Viewing Set (for lending to parents)		DD1015	$ 99.95		
8	"New Teacher" Behavior Management Kits K-4		See reverse for pricing			
8	"New Teacher" Behavior Management Kits 5-12		See reverse for pricing			
Available items not listed in catalog	Campuswide Discipline Management Packages		See reverse for pricing			
	Six-Point Plan for Raising Happy, Healthy Children		DD1016	$ 8.95		
	Ending the Homework Hassle		DD1017	$ 9.95		
	My Personal Dictionary (for PK-3 students)		DD1018	$ 1.00		

Shipping & Handling (Minimum $5)

Orders under	$250	add	10%
Orders over	$250	add	9%
Orders over	$1,000	add	8%
Orders over	$5,000	add	6%

Subtotal	
$________ x ____%	Minimum $5.00
Total	

School/District:______________________________ P.O. #____________

Name:______________________________ Day Phone:____________

Credit Card: ❑ VISA ❑ MASTERCARD

Address:______________________________ Credit Card #:____________

City:____________ State______ Zip________ Expiration Date:____________

What is the **value** of a consistent, campuswide, discipline plan? **Priceless!**
What is the **cost** of a consistent, campuswide, discipline plan? From **$29.24 per person!**

Campuswide Discipline Management Packages

Order Worksheet

Item #	Item	Qty	Qty	x	Price	Extension
DD1001	*Vision Management©* Text	1/teacher	____	x	$ 24.95	________
DD1005	Poster - Classroom Dedication	1/teacher	____	x	$ 2.25	________
DD1006	Poster - Management Plan	1/teacher	____	x	$ 2.25	________
DD1008	*Day2Day©* Volume 1 or 2	1/campus	____	x	$ 29.95	________
DD1012	*VISIONS Character-Building Binder©*	1/campus	____	x	$249.95	________
DD1013	Dividers for *VISIONS Binder©* Copies	1/teacher	____	x	$ 2.00	________

Quick Quote

1. Place the number of staff to receive materials here ______
2. Multiply that number by $31.45 and place here ✏ $____.__
3. Now, add $279.90 (for # 1008 & 1012) $ 279.90
4. Add to get the subtotal $____.__
5. Call the office for a shipping quote or calculate from the other side

As Budget Permits, Include These Key Components, Too!

Item #	Item	Qty	Qty	x	Price	Extension
DD1010	*Goal For It! K-4©*	1/teacher	___	x	$ 19.95	________
DD1011	*Goal For It! 5-12©*	1/teacher	___	x	$ 14.95	________
DD1014	*"911 for Parents"©* Video Training Kit	1/campus	___	x	$329.95	________

"New Teacher" Behavior Management Kits

How would you like all of your new teachers to start the year with:

- *A consistent, modern discipline plan*
- *A proven method to establish classroom discipline*
- *A desktop reference guide that handles 72 of the toughest classroom situations*

New Teacher Resource Pack (K-4) includes:

- *Vision Management©* Workbook Text
- *Goal For It!©* K-4 Behavior Book with puppets
- *Desktop Mentor©* Behavior Guide
- Management Plan Poster
- Teacher Dedication Poster
- Pencil Holder

New Teacher Resource Pack (Gr.5-12) includes:

- *Vision Management©* Workbook Text
- *Goal For It!©* 5-12 Behavior Book
- *Desktop Mentor©* Behavior Guide
- Management Plan Poster
- Teacher Dedication Poster
- Pencil Holder

Order 1 Pack for
- **$66.35 each + shipping**

Order 5+ for $59.95*/ea.
- Save 10%

Order 10+ for $54.95*/ea.
- Save 17%

Order 25+ for $49.95*/ea.
- Save 25%
- Includes FREE "Vision Study Guide" for teacher study groups

Order 100+ for $44.95*/ea.
- Save 32%
- Includes FREE "Vision Study Guide" for teacher study groups
- PLUS a FREE two hour phone consultation with your administrative team, site-based team or all teachers with resource packs

*shipping charges additional

Order 250+ for $39.50*/ea.
- Save 40%
- Includes FREE "Vision Study Guide" for teacher study groups
- PLUS a FREE two hour phone consultation with your administrative team, site-based team or all teachers with resource packs

-OR-

- A FREE 1/2-day in-service for all teachers receiving resource packs (expenses additional)